Seafood Fiesta

Seafood Fiesta

Katy Dalal

Vakils, Feffer and Simons Pvt. Ltd.
Industry Manor, 2nd Floor, Appasaheb Marathe Marg
Prabhadevi, Mumbai 400 025, India

First printing 2006

Price in India Rs. 295/-

Published by
Bimal Mehta for Vakils, Feffer and Simons Pvt. Ltd.
Industry Manor, Appasaheb Marathe Marg, Prabhadevi, Mumbai 400 025. India

Printed by
Arun K. Mehta at Vakil & Sons Private Ltd.
Industry Manor, Appasaheb Marathe Marg, Prabhadevi, Mumbai 400 025. India

Photographs by
Jamshed Billimoria

ISBN No.: 81-87111-74-7

This book is dedicated to my children — gourmets all — who have been my staunchest supporters and my severest critics.

My eldest son Kurush, who has done me proud by following my footsteps into Archaeology and Catering.

My daughter Freny, a Tourist Guide par excellence, fluent in French and with a love for India that makes her a favorite with tourists, as she unfolds the country's glories to them.

My youngest son Darius, a Solicitor by profession, who with his ever smiling face and gentle demeanour, provides a perfect counterpoint to my volatile and impatient nature.

Cover: Salmon Fillets in Lemon-Butter with Oak leaf salad

Colour Plates facing page Nos. 24, 32, 58, 59, 74, 75, 89 by courtesy of Bharat-Excellensea Restaurant

Contents

Introduction

People in general know so little about fish that I thought it would be appropriate to write a small introduction on what fish products can do. Besides being eaten, fish products are used in medicine.

I have relied very heavily on K. Devadasan's paper, "Fish-based Pharmaceuticals and Nutraceuticals and their Applications" as published in the International Symposium on Fish For Nutritional Security In the 21st Century, held between 4-6 December, 2001, Mumbai, India. I am extremely grateful to Mr. Devadasan for his article.

Wherever possible, when I am giving recipes of a particular fish, I try to give some information on it. The data on sardines, squids and octopus which are widely eaten, is fascinating.

Fish is eaten throughout the world. There are hundreds of types of fish but humans tend to eat only a few of them.

P. V. Dehadrai has written an extremely erudite article on "Nutrition Security Through Fisheries and Aquaculture in India".

In it he emphasizes the importance of fish as a source of high quality food. Fish provides most of the gross and essential proteins, fats, minerals, vitamins and essential amino acids. Polyunsaturated (PUFA) account for about 15.25% of the total fatty acids and EPA and DHA together account for about 90% of the total PUFA. These constituents are known to reduce serum cholesterol levels and prevent excessive platelet formation.

Fish is not only "brain food", it is excellent for the growth and development of the human body. Eating fish prevents some nutritional deficiencies such as protein energy malnutrition, B complex and Iodine deficiencies. Fish eating also reduces cancer risks.

The Times of India dated 6/2/04 carried a report from Tokyo about a 19-year old health study on fish. The report proved that people who eat fish regularly, live longer than others who don't eat fish regularly. The study showed a 30% reduction of death from heart disease and stroke in those persons who ate fish regularly.

K. Devadasan, in his paper at the Symposium, said that the world has become conscious that "Sea Food is Heart Food" and many people the world over are making a special effort to eat fish more often than before.

Eating fish is beneficial to heart patients. The "polyunsaturated fatty acids in fish oils are the main ingredients which are responsible for this beneficial effect of dietary fish."

The two main cardio-vascular problems are: (1) deposits of cholesterol on the inner walls of coronary arteries and (2) thrombotic problems leading to blood clots because of increased platelets. The polyunsaturated fatty acids of fish oils are "good remedies" for the eradication of both these problems.

People in different parts of the world who eat more of dietary fish are known to have less cardio-vascular problems. The Omega-3 group polyunsaturated fatty acids are the precursors of prostaglandins, prostacyclins and thromboxanes, which play a vital role in determining the rate of platelet aggregation.

The Omega-3 fatty acids also play an important part in the development of children's brain cells. In the pure unoxidised state they are known to have anti-carcinogenic properties.

Shark and cod liver oil are very good sources for natural Vitamins A and D. Of the several species of sharks available in Indian waters, only a few are commercially viable. According to a Japanese scholar, Tanikawa, Japan produces insulin from fish and whales. Tuna pancreas have more percentage of insulin than cattle.

Products from prawn waste are a valuable part of fish study. The technology for producing a "protein extract called CHITIN or CHITOSAN, from prawn waste has been worked out and successfully commercialized by the Central Institute of Fisheries Technology, in Cochin".

This installation has developed a process of creating Chitin from prawn shell waste which is found to be useful in antibiotics and baby food formulae. This is also used in broiler food for chickens. Its use was seen to "improve feed efficiency" which brought about a 10% to 12% weight gain when compared to a Chitin-free diet.

Chitosan is an invaluable chemical substance and is used in different ways. It can be used:

1. as a sizing material for textiles

2. to clarify wine or water

3. in preparing cosmetics

4. Chitosan if made into a micro-fined powder can "impregnate" gauze and film for treatment of chronic wounds, ulcers and leads to minimized bleeding in neurosurgery.

5. It is also used as artificial skin and kidney membrane and as contact lenses.

6. From being an enrivonmental problem, the prawn shell waste has turned into an important industrial raw material.

Collagens from the skin and air bladder of fish are used in (1) dentistry; (2) they are also used as artificial skin; (3) Chitosan impregnated collagen films are effective in reducing blood loss, fluid loss and prevent infection when used as artificial skin; (4) they do not produce any allergic tissue reactions.

Fish guts yield fine grade absorbable sutures for use in surgery.

Shark bones make up 10% to 15% of its body weight. Formerly only a very small amount of bones were used to make buttons and necklaces. Now, new research has found that the cartilege is rich in chondroitin sulphate which is useful in medicine for the treatment of arteriosclerosis, blood vessel thrombosis, and also helps to prevent infections. Shark bones are in demand in Europe, U.S.A. and Australia.

The fin rays of the shark are exported from India. The rays are used to make soup in Asian countries.

Tuna eyes are a commercial item as it contains polyunsaturated fatty acids. Its medical properties are useful to combat arteriosclerotic and thrombotic problems of chronic heart patients. It is said to be anti-carcinogenic. It helps to develop the brain.

Calcium Powder made from tuna backbone helps fight calcium deficiency in children. It prevents bone failure and spine curvature.

Beche-de-mer is the commercial name for sea cucumbers. These are dried and exported from India. To the Chinese, it is an aphrodisiac. It is useful in the treatment of high blood pressure.

Ambergris which is a secretion from male sperm whales, is extremely valuable and is used in blending exotic perfumes. It is found on sea shores of countries like India, Australia, New Zealand and the Bahamas in large fragments or as a "whole mass". The current value of Ambergris is Rs. 50,000 per kg.

Fish Meal is a highly concentrated nutritious feed supplement. It is made up of high quality protein, minerals, vitamin B and other "factors". It is produced by cooking, pressing, drying and grinding the bony remains of fish along with its tissues which are full of protein. This is available through canning processors from fish such as sole, silver bellies, ribbon fish and jew fish caught along with prawns.

Squid Meal made out of squid offal, is reported to have growth promoting effects on farmed fish. A 30% to 40% growth improvement has been seen in shrimp growing. The Ink Sac in the mantle cavity contains a dark coloured liquid called "ink". In Japan, it has been used for generations as a preservative and flavour enhancer.

Squid ink has preservative and anti-oxidant values as well as anti-cancer properties.

Acknowledgements

This book was a real pleasure to write. I have provided generally favourite recipes mostly on fish which is easily available to the public.

I am very grateful to Dr. Boman Chhapgar, Marine Biologist, former Curator of Taraporevala Aquarium, Mumbai for his valuable advice and for kindly agreeing to release this book and to Dr. Vinay Deshmukh, Officer-in-charge, Central Marine Fisheries Research Institute, Mumbai for all the information and guidance he provided.

I am highly indebted to Mr. Sangram Sawant, Managing Director, Pesca Fresh for sponsoring this book.

I thank Mr. Suraj Salian, proprietor of the restaurant "Bharat-Excellensea" for allowing me to photograph a number of their excellent fish dishes.

I also thank Miss Parviz Dungor who typed the manuscript so diligently and Mr. Jamshed Billimoria for the beautiful pictures he has taken.

But more than anything, I would like to thank Ms. Sangeeta Bhansali and dear Katey Cooper of Vakils for the care and thoughts expended on this book.

Sincerely,

Katy Dalal

Masala, Sauces and Various Fish Butters

To Make Fish Stock

Ingredients

2 kgs (approx.) Fish heads, bones, trimmings
10 cups water
2 cups carrots, chopped
2 cups onions, chopped
½ cup celery stalks, chopped

¼ cup parsley stalks, chopped
½ cup white wine
3 bay leaves
4 thyme sprigs
16 crushed black peppercorns
Salt

Method

1.   Place all the above items, except the black peppercorns in a large vessel and allow the liquid to boil. Remove the scum which will form on top. Simmer for 30 minutes. Cool. Strain the liquid through a fine sieve. Discard the bones and vegetables.

2.   Pour into plastic bags. Seal and freeze until needed.

Mayonnaise

Ingredients

3 eggs
4 tsps sugar
4 tsps white vinegar or lime juice
½ tsp pepper powder

½ tsp mustard powder (optional)
1½ kgs refined oil
Salt

Method

1.   Place all ingredients except oil, in a mixer and blend at a low speed and simultaneously add the oil in a slow trickle till the mayonnaise becomes thick and forms peaks.

2.   Store an airtight glass bottle and chill.

Tandoori Masala

Ingredients

For 12 Pomfrets

For the 1st marinade
10 gms aji-no-moto
Juice of 3 sour limes
Salt

For the 2nd marinade
500 gms whipped thick yoghurt
25 gms raw mango powder
2 tbsps jalebi colour
3 tbsps ghee
4 iron skewers

For the ground masala paste

(Grind to a fine paste with 1 cup sugarcane vinegar)
100 gms Kashmiri chillies
50 gms tamarind
25 gms skinned garlic cloves
10 gms cinnamon
10 gms cloves

Method

1. Clean the pomfrets, scale them, remove the gills and intestines by making a cut above the stomach from the side. Wash well.

2. Salt the pomfrets, make 3 diagonal cuts on each side. Apply the lime juice and the aji-no-moto and marinade for an hour or two.

3. In a vessel, whisk the yoghurt, jalebi colour and the mango powder. Then mix in the ground masala and coat the pomfrets well with the mixture. Marinade overnight in a refrigerator.

4. The next day, half an hour before serving, light a charcoal fire and allow the coals to turn white. Fix one pomfret on each skewer and place them across the hot coals. Keep turning the fish and applying a little ghee dabbed on a piece of muslin until evenly roasted.

5. Serve with green chillies, sliced onion rings and wedges of sour lime.

Green Sauce

Ingredients

1 bunch spinach, washed well
½ bunch coriander, washed well
¼ cup parsley, finely chopped

1 tsp fresh ginger, grated
2 cups mayonnaise
Salt

Method

1. Grind the greens, ginger and salt in a liquidizer.
2. Blend the ground mixture with the mayonnaise.

Tartare Sauce

Ingredients

3 cups mayonnaise
¼ cup capsicum, finely chopped
½ cup celery stalks, finely chopped
½ cup white of cucumbers, finely chopped
¼ cup spring onions, finely chopped

2 tbsps parsley, finely chopped
½ cup tomato sauce
1 tsp tabasco sauce
½ tsp white pepper powder
Salt

Method

1. Place all the above items in a large glass bowl. Mix gently and chill.

Hot and Spicy Tomato Sauce

Ingredients

700 gms fresh tomato pulp
1 large onion, finely chopped
1 red pepper, finely chopped
2 bay leaves
1 tsp sugar
¼ cup finely chopped parsley

2 green chillies, deseeded and finely chopped
1 tsp red chilli powder
Salt
2 tbsps refined oil

Method

1.   Heat the oil over a medium flame in a large saucepan. Add the bay leaves and onions and allow them to turn pink and translucent. Add the peppers, green chillies and the chilli powder.

2.   Add the tomato pulp and bring to a boil. Taste for salt.

3.   Add the sugar and the parsley. Mix well, cook for 3 more minutes and remove from the heat.

4.   Serve either hot or cold.

Mustard Sauce

Ingredients

2 tbsps French mustard   1 cup cream
Juice of 1 sour lime   Salt
½ tsp white pepper powder

Method

1.   Mix mustard, lemon juice, salt and pepper in a bowl.

2.   Whip the cream and stir in the mustard mixture.

3.   Chill and serve with steamed oysters or fish.

Mornay Sauce Hollandaise

Ingredients

3 egg yolks   1½ cups butter
1 tbsp white wine vinegar   2-3 tbsps water
1 tbsp sour lime juice   Salt
6 crushed black peppercorns

Method

1.   Make this sauce in a double boiler or an oven-proof bowl over a saucepan of hot water.

2.   Place the white wine vinegar, peppercorns and water into a small saucepan and allow it to boil down to 1 tablespoon of liquid.

3. Gently melt the butter.

4. Place egg yolks, reduced liquid and a little melted butter into the double boiler.

5. Whisk the mixture till it becomes creamy. Then gently add the rest of the butter whisking all the time. Add the lemon juice and salt.

6. Remove from heat and serve immediately with fish fillets or steamed fish.

7. Add whipped cream to this sauce to get MOUSSELINE SAUCE.

Lime and Chilli Sauce

Ingredients

Juice of 5 sour limes

8 egg yolks, whisked

6 green chillies, deseeded and
ground to a pulp

250 gms butter, melted

Salt

Method

1. Place all the items in a saucepan, taste for salt, and place it over a slightly bigger saucepan half-filled with water.

2. Put the saucepan over medium heat. Take a slim wooden spoon and gently rotate the mixture non-stop till it slowly begins to thicken and turn glossy.

3. Remove from the fire and turn the sauce out in a glass bowl.

Bechamel Sauce

Ingredients

1 litre milk

½ cup butter

50 gms refined flour

1 onion, chopped into 4 pieces

1 mace flower

1 tbsp parsley, finely chopped

5 peppercorns

1 bay leaf

White pepper powder

Salt

Method

1. Place the milk in a pan along with the onion, bay leaf, peppercorns, mace and parsley. Warm over a low heat for 10 minutes. Do not boil. Cover and allow to stand for 10 minutes.

2. Melt the butter gently over a low heat. Add the flour and continue to mix till smooth.

3. Add milk in a slow trickle to the butter and flour and blend to get a thick white sauce. Season with salt and pepper.

4. If you make this sauce with stock and wine, it becomes VELOUTE SAUCE.

Hariyali Sauce

Ingredients

1 large onion, finely ground
1 cup coriander leaves
1 cup spinach leaves, chopped
Juice of 2 sour limes
2 tbsps sugar
Salt
2 tbsps refined oil

For the ground masala paste

(Grind fine with a little water)
6 cloves garlic
4-6 green chillies, deseeded
1 tbsp cumin seeds
1 tsp coriander seeds
1 tsp fennels seeds
7 black peppercorns

Method

1. Put the oil in a saucepan and cook the onion till pink but not brown. Boil the coriander and spinach leaves with a pinch of soda-bi-carb, then grind fine, add to the onion and cook for 3 minutes. Then add the ground masala and salt and allow to cook for 5 minutes over a low flame.

2. Add as much water as needed and mix in the sugar and lemon juice and stir well for 2 minutes. Remove from the fire.

Ginger and Wine Sauce for Clams

Method

1. Place the cleaned, washed clams in a large pot of boiling, salted water.

2. Add crushed ginger, crushed garlic, cut red dried chillies and pepper powder.

3. When the clams have cooked and opened out, drain the stock through a fine sieve.

4. Return to the fire and reduce the quantity. Then add 1 cup of red or white wine and simmer 5 minutes. Serve hot.

Anchovy Butter

Ingredients

6 anchovy fillets
2 tbsps milk
½ cup butter

¼ tsp tabasco sauce
¼ tsp white pepper powder

Method

1. Soak the anchovy fillets in milk. Mash with a wooden spoon.

2. Add the butter, tabasco and pepper and mix well.

3. Chill.

Garlic Butter

Ingredients

1 cup butter
4 large cloves garlic, crushed fine
¼ cup parsley, finely chopped

2 tbsps sour lime juice
1 tsp white pepper powder
Salt

Method

1. Place butter and garlic in a blender and blend well.

2. Remove into a bowl and mix in the parsley, lime juice, salt and white pepper powder.

3. Chill.

Prawn and Chilli Butter

Ingredients

400 gms butter

400 gms deveined prawns, washed, salted, boiled and finely chopped

3 tbsps celery, finely chopped

2 tbsps green or red peppers, finely chopped

2 tsps sour lime juice

1 tsp green chillies, finely chopped

Salt

Method

1. Mix all the ingredients well and store in an airtight container. Chill.

2. Use within 3 days.

Fish Butter

Ingredients

300 gms salted butter

350 gms white fish flesh, boiled, deboned

2 tbsps parsley, minced

1 tbsp mint, minced

1 tbsp prepared mustard

1 tbsp thyme, chopped

Method

1. Shred the fish flesh.

2. Add butter and all the ingredients and mix well.

3. Chill.

Crab Butter

Ingredients

300 gms salted butter
350 gms fresh crab meat boiled
2 tbsps celery, chopped

2 tbsps red or green peppers
1 tsp black pepper, coarsely ground
2 tsps sour lime juice

Method

1. Mix all the items in a glass bowl.

2. Chill and serve with crackers or melba toast.

Hot Green Coconut Chutney

Preparation time: 30-45 mins   Serves: 6-11

Ingredients

1 large coconut, grated
15-20 cloves of garlic
6 green chillies, deseeded
1 tsp cumin seeds
Juice of 2 sour limes
1½ tsps sugar

1 tsp chopped mint
2 cups coriander leaves, washed and
chopped
½ tsp black pepper powder
Salt

Method

1. Grind all the ingredients very finely on a stone mortar or in a mixer. Add the sugar and lime juice last. Mix well. Serve.

Cleaning & Preparation

Preparing Squid

Method

1. Hold the base of the head and pull out the attached stomach portion from the sac. Discard the head and rinse the body thoroughly, inside and out.

2. Cut off all the tentacles below the eyes. Remove the "beak".

3. Remove the outer skin along with the "wings" until only milky white flesh remains.

4. Remove the cartilage that runs vertically along the body sac. Wash the hood again and cut into rings.

5. Boil the Squid rings. Coat the rings with a seasoned batter of flour, salt and water.

6. Fry till crisp and golden and serve hot.

Cleaning Mussels and Clams

Method

1. Place in water which has been salted so that they disgorge grit. Discard any that fail to open or are broken.

2. Scrub the mussels and crabs with a small stiff brush so that the barnacles and dirt will dislodge.

3. For mussels, remove the small hair-like strands which protrude from one side of the shell. This is called "bearding".

Cleaning Scallops

Method

1. Scallop shells can be a little difficult to open. If you buy scallops in their shells, push a sharp knife between the shells to open them. Take care not to cut the flesh inside.

2. Cut away the white flesh from the shell and remove the inedible portions. Discard them. Keep the coral whole.

3. Wash under running water to rinse away all sand and grit.

4. Remove the scallop and cook it in a sauce or grill or bake it in a sauce in the shell itself.

Cleaning Lobster

Method

1. The best way to cook a live lobster is to immerse it in boiling salted water. The second method is to hold the lobster steady with a napkin and with a heavy knife, cut through behind its head.

2. You can cut across the tail at its natural ridges to make wedges or medallions.

3. Another method is to cut the tail lengthwise down the center, creating two equal halves.

4. Remove the lobster's intestinal tract.

5. Separate the feelers from the body.

6. Cut the body section in half, lengthwise.

7. Remove and discard the gelatinous sac in the head, as it is dangerous to eat.

8. Wash the parts well and cook.

How to Boil Oysters, Clams and Lobsters

Method

1.   Place the oysters, clams or lobster in a large pot of water to boil. Add salt, crushed ginger, bay leaves and lime juice.

2.   Cook until tender.

How to Cook a Crab

Method

1.   Place the boiled, cooked crab on a wooden board.

2.   Twist the claws until they separate from the body. Crack them open with a hammer. Remove the white meat from the claws and place it in a bowl.

3.   Hold the crab in a strong grip with both hands, and with your thumbs push the body section away from the shell.

4.   Discard the small sac or stomach bag attached to the large shell. Rinse off green waste in the centre and remove the grey spongy parts known as the "dead man's fingers".

5.   Scrape the browny meat from the shell into a clean bowl.

6.   If using the shell for baking purposes, wash and scrub the insides and rinse well. Use no soap.

7.   Cook the white and brown meats as desired.

Anchoiade

The French people love anchovies and each home preserves the fresh catches in salt to last them year round. Anchovy paste is very popular with all the Mediterranean people.

Preparation time: 20 mins   Serves: 6-8

Ingredients

125 gms salted anchovies
4 garlic cloves
½ tsp black pepper, freshly ground

1 tbsp vinegar, red wine vinegar preferably
4 tbsps olive oil

Method

1.   Soak the salted anchovies in plain water for 12-15 minutes.
2.   De-bone the fish.
3.   Place the garlic cloves in a mortar along with the fish and ½ teaspoon of pepper powder. Using a pestle, mash into a fine paste.
4.   Slowly add olive oil, ½ teaspoon at a time into the paste and keep grinding with the pestle.
5.   Gently stir in the vinegar.
6.   Store in a pot with a lid.
7.   Serve, spread on a thin toast.

Anchovy Stuffed Peppers

Ingredients

6 golden peppers with stems attached
2 cans anchovy fillets
3 large cloves garlic, finely sliced
Chopped parsley

5 large red tomatoes, skinned and chopped
Olive oil
Salt

Method

1. Cut off the tops of the peppers and set aside. Cook in hot salted water for 5 to 7 minutes.

2. Place 2 tablespoons of olive oil in a frying pan over a moderate heat. Add the garlic and chopped tomatoes and cook till soft.

3. Add the anchovies, parsley and black pepper to the tomato mixture and cook for 3 minutes. Cool.

4. Stuff the mixture into the peppers and put back the sliced tops.

5. Grease a baking dish with butter and arrange the peppers on it. Add ½ cup of water and bake in a pre-heated oven at 400° F for 25 minutes.

6. Serve with French bread or Indian parathas.

Anchovy Hors-D'Oeuvres

Preparation time: 12 mins

Serves: 8

Ingredients

No. 1

8 tomatoes, scooped out

2 small tins anchovy fillets, mashed

2 tbsps parsley, finely chopped

4 hard boiled eggs, chopped small

2 large cucumbers, thinly sliced

1 large cup lettuce

Juice of 2 sour limes

Fresh ground black pepper

Salt

Method

1.   Arrange washed, dried lettuce leaves on a flat dish. Arrange salted cucumber slices in a circle.

2.   In a bowl, mash the anchovies and mix in the parsley, boiled eggs and black pepper to taste. Stuff this mixture into the empty tomatoes.

3.   Arrange the stuffed tomatoes on the bed of lettuce. Chill and serve.

No. 2

8 slices of toasted bread

6 hard boiled eggs, chopped

1 tin anchovy fillets

2 tbsps sour lime juice

Fresh ground black pepper

Salt

Butter

Method

1.   Place 1 cup butter in a bowl. Add 5 anchovy fillets, lime juice and black pepper to taste. Mash well.

2.   Apply the butter to the toast. Top with the chopped eggs and the anchovy fillets.

3.   Serve on a bed of finely chopped lettuce.

Indian Style Fried Golden Anchovies
(Mandela)

Preparation time: 15-20 mins   Cooking time: 10 mins   Serves: 5-7

Ingredients

500 gms golden anchovies
2 tbsps chilli powder
2 tbsps turmeric powder
Salt
Refined oil

Method

1.   Soak the fish in cold water.

2.   Place each on a wooden board and scrape off the tiny scales with a blunt knife. Cut off the heads diagonally so the entrails come off with the head. Wash well twice and separate into the tiny ones and the large ones. Sprinkle salt and the chilli and turmeric powders and set aside for 30 minutes.

3.   Heat oil in a frying pan. When very hot, immerse the tiny anchovies in the hot oil and fry in batches until crisp. Remove from the oil and place on paper towels. Eat these with their little bones all fried to a crisp.

4.   Fry the larger sized anchovies in hot oil till golden brown. Remove the central bone before eating.

5.   Serve as canapés or with rice and dal or vegetables and rotis.

The Bombay Duck

The Bombay Duck, name Harpodon Nehereus, is a major type of fish found along the coasts of Gujarat and Maharashtra. On an average, it makes up about 10% of the total fish caught in India. Only 2% of this fish comes from Andhra Pradesh, West Bengal and Orissa.

This fish should be cooked fast as it has poor keeping qualities. Because it is a very soft fish it rots quickly. Quite a lot of Bombay Ducks are therefore dried in the sun, after being salted, on bamboo scaffoldings. Whatever has gone bad is converted into manure.

In Marathi, this fish is called "bombil" and in Bengali, "Bumaloh".

Its body is long, soft and gelatinous. It has a large head and small eyes and a wide deep mouth. It has recurved, depressible teeth in its jaws, enlarged in the lower jaws. The scales start halfway between the snout and the root of the caudel. Its colour is pinkish near the mouth and head and greyish-white in the body.

The Bombay Duck eats prawns. As the fish matures, its diet is supplemented by other fish.

It is an indiscriminative feeder. It is carnivorous and cannilbalistic.

Fried Masala Bombay Ducks

Preparation time: 12 mins   Cooking time: 30 mins   Serves: 6

Ingredients

20 dried Bombay Ducks,
cleaned, cut into 4 to 6 pieces
each and soaked in water
for ½ hour
1 large onion, finely chopped
Salt
Peanut oil

For the ground masala paste

6 green chillies, deseeded
½ cup coriander leaves, washed
4 curry leaves
1" piece ginger
5 large cloves garlic
1 tbsp cumin
Juice of 3 sour limes

Method

1.   Dry the soaked Bombay Duck pieces with a soft kitchen paper.

2.   Heat oil in a deep frying pan and deep fry the fish in small batches till crisp. Drain on a paper napkin.

3.   Drain away excess oil and in the same pan, sautée the onions till soft and pink. Add the ground masala and cook well over a very low flame. Taste for salt.

4.   Add the fried Bombay Duck and stir well, till fish is evenly coated and flavours have blended. Heat through for 4 minutes. Squeeze or sprinkle the lime juice on top and serve.

Akoori with Dried Bombay Ducks

Preparation time: 20 mins   Cooking time: 20 mins   Serves: 6

Ingredients

2 large dried Bombay Ducks
8 eggs
2 large onions, sliced and deep fried
4 green chillies, deseeded and finely cut
½ bunch fresh coriander, finely chopped
½ tsp ginger-garlic paste

¼ tsp turmeric powder
½ tsp chilli powder
2 tbsps ghee
Salt
Oil

Method

1.   Soak the Bombay Ducks in water for an hour. Remove the centre bone and shred into tiny pieces. Wash twice and drain. Pat dry with a soft clean cloth. Deep fry in hot oil and place on absorbent paper.

2.   Place 2 tablespoons ghee in a pan and add the chillies, coriander, garlic-ginger paste and spices and cook for 2 minutes. Add the fried onions and stir for 2 more minutes over a low flame.

3.   Whip the eggs well, add salt to taste and pour it into the onion mixture. Stir vigorously for 2 to 3 minutes. As the egg mixture, thickers, add the fried Bombay Ducks. Turn off the heat. Mix well and serve hot with rice flour chapatis.

Filleted Bombay Ducks with Green Coconut Chutney

Preparation time: 20-25 mins   Cooking time: 25-30 mins   Serves: 6-8

Ingredients

20 fresh Bombay Ducks
(cleaned well, skin gently
scrubbed for scales,
heads and tails cut off and
the stomach portion cut
and cleansed)
1-2 tbsp chilli powder

¾ tbsp turmeric powder
1 hot green coconut chutney
(pg. 10)
1 cup gram flour
Salt
Oil

Method

1.   Wash each Bombay Duck and slit it from the top to the bottom on the stomach side. Lay the fillet flat and remove the single central bone.

2.   Mix turmeric, chilli powder and salt and rub the masala well into the flesh.

3.   Apply the green coconut chutney on one side of the fillet and fold over to resemble whole Bombay Duck.

4.   Mix gram flour, salt and water to make a batter thick enough to coat the slippery flesh.

5.   Heat enough oil in a frying pan.

6.   Dip the Bombay Ducks into the batter, fry 5 to 6 Bombay Ducks in a row in the pan. Turn over gently once they are golden brown, and fry the other side. Remove and drain on kitchen paper.

7.   Do not allow the oil to overheat or the Bombay Ducks will get burnt. While frying Bombay Duck care needs to be taken to avoid breaking the tender flesh.

8.   Serve hot garnished with slices of limes and soft bread.

Fresh Bombay Duck Curry

Preparation time: 18-20 mins   Cooking time: 25-30 mins   Serves: 6-8

Ingredients

12 large tail pieces of Bombay Ducks or
20 whole baby Bombay Ducks,
1½ coconuts fresh milk
2 large onions, finely chopped
3 large tomatoes, skinned and
finely chopped
6 kokum pieces
Salt
½ cup peanut oil

For the ground masala paste

12-14 green chillies, deseeded
½ cup grams, skinned
1 ½ tbsps cumin seeds
12 large cloves garlic
5 black peppercorns
½ cup coriander

Method

1.   Apply salt over the cleaned Bombay Duck and keep aside.

2.   Fry the onions in oil in a thick, flat-bottomed vessel, till soft and pink.

3.   Add the ground masala and stir for 5 minutes over a low heat. When cooked, add the tomatoes and allow them to soften stirring all the time. Then add the coconut milk and bring to a fast boil. Add the kokum.

4.   Add the Bombay Ducks to the gravy and cook for 5 minutes over a high flame. Taste for salt. Simmer for a few more minutes.

5.   Serve hot with rice and papad.

Fresh Bombay Duck Curry
– Saraswat Style

Preparation time: 15 mins   Cooking time: 25 mins   Serves: 6

Ingredients

12 semi-large Bombay Ducks
¾ tsp turmeric powder
½ cup thick tamarind water
2 sprigs curry leaves
Salt
½ cup of peanut or coconut oil

For the ground masala paste

½ fresh coconut, grated
8 green chillies, deseeded
2" fresh ginger, grated
12 large cloves garlic
7 black peppercorns
¼ cup coriander leaves
½ onion, finely chopped

Method

1.   Wash and clean the Bombay Ducks and cut each into 2 to 3 pieces according to their size. Salt and set aside.

2.   Apply turmeric to the fish.

3.   Heat ½ cup of oil in a heavy, flat-bottomed vessel. Add the masala to the hot oil and stir for 3 minutes. Add the tamarind water and stir well and allow the mixture to come to a boil.

4.   Add the curry leaves and then the Bombay Duck pieces. Do not stir with a spoon. Hold the vessel with kitchen napkins in both your hands and stir it up and down for 7 minutes, till the fish is cooked. Taste for salt.

5.   Serve with boiled rice and papads. Since this curry does not contain much liquid, it can be eaten with chapatis or rotis also.

Bekti in Saffron Sauce

Preparation time: 10 mins   Cooking time: 25-30 mins   Serves: 6

Ingredients

10 Bekti fillets, each 3" by 2"
1 large onion, finely chopped
1 gm saffron
7 green chillies, deseeded and
chopped fine
1 cup fresh tomato puree
1 tsp paprika

1 tsp powdered cumin
3 tbsps cashewnut paste
2 tbsps fresh coriander leaves
1 tsp sugar
Salt
Pure ghee

Method

1.   Wash and salt the fish. Set aside.

2.   Place 3 tablespoons of ghee in a flat-bottomed vessel and sauté the chopped onion.

3.   Add the green chillies, paprika, cumin and cashewnut paste and stir well. Add the tomato puree and allow to simmer. Add the sugar.

4.   Heat the saffron on a tava and crumble it into ½ cup of hot water. Mix well.

5.   Add the saffron water and salt to the gravy. Add the bekti and bring to a boil. Lower the flame and simmer for 7 minutes.

6.   Garnish with the freshly chopped coriander.

7.   Serve with steamed rice or bread slices.

Top: Mangalorean Prawn Ghassi
Below: Filleted Bombay Ducks
Left: Appam ❯

Bourride:
Provençal Fish Soup with Garlic Mayonnaise

Preparation time: 40 mins   Cooking time: 30 mins   Serves: 6

Ingredients

For the Court Bouillon:

1 kg head of fish and bones
2½ litres water
2 brown onions, halved and sliced into half moons
4 spring onions
1 tbsp orange peel, grated
3 bay leaves
1 tbsp fennel seeds
2 tbsps white wine vinegar or white vinegar
Salt

For the Aioli:

8-10 garlic cloves, finely sliced
7 egg yolks
Juice of 1 sour lime
1 tsp white pepper
1 tbsp dried breadcrumbs
1 tbsp white wine vinegar
1¼ cups olive oil

For the Fish:

1 kg fish fillets of white fish such as salmon, ghol or surmai each cut into 2" squares

Croutes:

12 slices French bread

Method

1. In a large vessel, put in the washed fish heads, washed bones, herbs, onions, wine, vinegar, fennel seeds, orange peel and salt. Allow to boil over a hot stove. Then place on low heat and simmer for ½ hour.

2. Soak the breadcrumbs in 1 tablespoon of wine vinegar for 5-7 minutes. Then squeeze the liquid from the crumbs with a cloth napkin.

3. Place the garlic pods along with the crumbs into a large mortar and mash both with a pestle until you have a smooth paste.

4. In a soup plate, beat 3 egg yolks with a fork or wire whisk and add them a little at a time to the garlic paste. Add salt and pepper powder. Empty into a

◄ Bourride

large bowl. When the mixture has become gluey, add the olive oil, 1 teaspoon at a time, and beat it in with a wire whisk or electric beater. You should get a creamy liquid. Add the lime juice. Mix and taste for salt and pepper. Now pour 1 cup of the mixture into a small bowl or sauce-boat and cover with foil. Whatever remains should be poured into a large saucepan or vessel.

5.   Strain the court bouillon through a sieve or cloth piece into a bowl. Try and squeeze as much essence as you can from the herbs by pressing them with a spoon before discarding them and the soup bones.

6.   Wash the pan in which the bouillon was boiled and put the fish fillets into it. Then pour over the strained bouillon and simmer the whole over a medium flame for about 10 minutes until the fish is cooked but firm. Transfer the cooked fish pieces onto a pyrex dish and keep warm by covering it.

7.   Beat the 4 egg yolks that are left, one at a time into the aioli which we had placed in a large saucepan. Add 1 cup of the hot bouillon into it beating it with a wire whisk. Slowly beat in all the fish soup. Cook over a low heat stirring all the time until the soup coats the back of your spoon. Taste for salt, pepper, and lemon and add more if you need it.

8.   When you are ready to eat, pour the soup into a large tureen. Place the fish pieces in a flat dish, decorated with parsley and iceberg lettuce. Place the little bowl on the table also. Keep the 12 pieces of French bread hot and toasted.

9.   To eat, serve the soup in a soup plate after putting one slice of the croute on the bottom. Then place one or two pieces of fish on the croute and top it with a small ladle of aioli.

10. Serve as much soup as the guests want. Keep extra croutes ready to hand.

11. Bourride is a delicious meal in itself. Follow it with fresh fruits and ice-cream.

Baked Bhing Roe Pie

Preparation time: 7 mins   Cooking time: 30-35 mins   Serves: 6

Ingredients

1 large Bhing roe, washed, and both pieces boiled in salted water containing green chillies and coriander

½ cup cheese, grated

6 large potatoes, boiled, salted, mashed and seasoned with salt and butter

½ litre white sauce (mixed with sautéed mushrooms)

Salt

Butter

Method

1. Drain the roe, and cut into slices. Fry lightly in butter. Arrange in a medium sized buttered dish.

2. Pour the white sauce.

3. Pipe the mashed potato mixture around the dish.

4. Sprinkle cheese on top of the sauce and bake at 450° F till golden on top.

Bengali Rohu or Carp Roe Fritters

Preparation time: 18 mins   Cooking time: 25 mins   Serves: 4-6

Ingredients

1 side of a carp roe
1½" ground ginger
2 medium onions, chopped fine
2½ tsps turmeric powder
6 green chillies, deseeded and
chopped fine
½ cup mint leaves, finely chopped
Juice of 2 limes

2 tsps sugar
1 large boiled potato, mashed
2½ tbsps maida or self-raising flour
1 tsp cumin, powdered
10 curry leaves, chopped
Salt
Refined oil

Method

1.   Wash the roe and remove the membrane. Mash the roe in a bowl.

2.   Mix all the ingredients with the roe. Add salt to taste.

3.   Place a deep frying pan half filled with oil on a medium flame. Drop tablespoons of the batter into the hot oil and fry till golden brown.

4.   These fritters can be eaten as a snack or together with dal and rice.

Bengali Rui Maccher Doi Maach

Preparation time: 15-18 mins   Cooking time: 25-30 mins   Serves: 6

Ingredients

6-8 large pieces of Rui or Carp

3 bay leaves or 3 sprigs curry leaves

1 onion, sliced

200 gms curds

4 split green chillies

1 tbsp sugar

Salt

Oil/Ghee

For the ground masala paste

For dry masala

2" piece cinnamon

3 green cardamoms (seeds only)

2 cloves

1/2" piece turmeric

8 Kashmiri chillies, deseeded

2 onions ground

2" ginger piece

8 large cloves garlic

Method

1. Wash the fish and salt it.

2. Heat oil/ghee in a pan and lightly fry the fish.

3. Take a large flat-bottomed vessel. Add 3 tablespoons oil from what is left in the frying pan. Place on medium heat.

4. Add the bay leaves, sliced onions and the ground masala. Stir well for 3 minutes. Add ¼ cup water and the ground onions. Allow the mixture to simmer, stirring all the while. Add the green chillies.

5. Add the fried fish carefully to the gravy and allow to simmer.

6. Whisk the curds with a pinch of salt and ½ cup water and add it to the fish. Simmer for a few more minutes till gravy thickens.

7. Serve hot with khichdi and a green salad.

The Crabs

Crabs are included in the sub-order Brachyura. The body is covered by a hard chitinous, partly calcified carapace. It has 5 pairs of head appendages or feelers, and 8 pairs of thoracic appendages. The last 5 pairs are the legs. The first pair of these legs are powerful and are used for grasping food and for serving as defensive organs. The rest are used for walking or swimming.

Crabs are rich in variety of species. They occupy marine, estuarine or brackish water.

A few species live in close association with other organisms. For instance, the pinnotherid crabs live in the mangle cavity of several types of bi-valve molluscs.

The Indian waters have over 600 species of crabs. There is no large fishery for them. Crabs support a small fishery and are mostly collected by poor, coastal people for personal use.

Some species are highly nutritious and are as delicious as lobsters or prawns. Their flesh is sweet.

Devilled Crab, Indian Style

Preparation time: 15-20 mins   Cooking time: 30 mins   Serves: 6-8

Ingredients

6 large crabs cleaned and boiled in water with salt and cut celery
1 tbsp readymade mustard
½ cup fresh breadcrumbs
2 tbsps Worcester sauce

2 tbsps cream
4 green chillies, deseeded and chopped fine
Salt
Butter

Method

1.   Retain the upper shell and remove the meat from the body section.

2.   Place in a bowl and mix in the breadcrumbs, Worcester sauce, green chillies, salt, black pepper, mustard and the cream. Mix well and replace in the crab shells or put the mixture in a buttered pyrex dish.

3.   Top with some more breadcrumbs mixed in melted butter and brown under a grill or heat in the oven at 400°F.

Steamed Crab with Butter Sauce

Preparation time: 15 mins   Cooking time: 10 mins   Serves: 2-4

Ingredients

1 large crab
Juice of 2 sour limes
1" ginger, finely sliced
1 bay leaf
200 gms pure butter
2 tsps ginger, minced

3 tsps garlic, minced
2 fresh green chillies, deseeded and finely chopped
1 tsp chilli oil
Salt

Method

1.   Clean the crab, crack the claws and cut the body into required pieces. Salt lightly and place in a heavy-bottomed pan. Add 2 cups of water, the sour lime juice and the sliced ginger and bay leaf. Allow to cook over a moderate flame till the flesh is tender. Drain off the excess water.

2.   Place the butter into a saucepan along with the minced ginger and garlic and cook gently along with the fresh green chilli oil. Cook stirring till the sauce is thick and the ginger, garlic and chillies are well mashed. Taste for salt. Serve in a separate bowl along with the crab.

*Steamed Crab with
Butter Sauce* ❯

Crab Scallops

Preparation time: 10 mins   Cooking time: 18-20 mins   Serves: 6

Ingredients

2 large boiled crabs, cleaned and sliced
1 cup mayonnaise
½ cup cheese, grated
2 tbsps Tabasco sauce
½ cup breadcrumbs
Butter

Method

1. Mix the crab meat, mayonnaise and tabasco sauce well in a glass bowl.
2. Divide between 6 buttered scallop shells or small pyrex bowls.
3. Sprinkle with breadcrumbs, cheese and dollops of butter.
4. Bake at 350°F till the tops are crisp.
5. Serve with french fries and lettuce salad.

‹ *Fish Fillets with
piquant Orange Sauce*

Crab and Pineapple Curry

Preparation time: 20-25 mins   Cooking time: 35 mins   Serves: 6-8

Ingredients

4 big size crabs
1 large ripe pineapple
½ fresh coconut, milk extracted
½ tsp mustard seeds
2 sprigs curry leaves
4 slit green chillies
Salt
½ cup peanut or coconut oil

For the ground masala paste
(Grind fine with ½ cup of water)
½ fresh coconut, grated
1 onion, finely chopped
2" thick piece lemon grass
½ cup coriander leaves, chopped
10 Kashmiri chillies
1 tbsp broiled coriander seeds
1 tsp broiled aniseeds
1½" fresh turmeric or 1" dry piece

Method

1.   Immerse crabs in salted boiling water for 15 mins and clean as explained on pg. 13. Cut each large centre into 4 equal pieces.

2.   Cut the pineapple vertically downwards in 4 long pieces so as to eliminate the central core. Dice the fruit into 1" chunks, while retaining any of the juice.

3.   Heat oil in a large vessel and add mustard seeds, curry leaves and green chillies.

4.   Add the ground masala and fry it well over a low flame. Add 1 cup water and bring the gravy to boil. Toss in the crab and cook, covered for 10 minutes. Add the coconut milk extract and the pineapple chunks and simmer for another 10 minutes. Taste for salt and remove from the fire.

5.   Serve hot with basmati rice, spicy frenchbeans, fried anchovies and papads.

Tamil Crab Curry
(Nandu Kari Kozhambu)

Preparation time: 20-25 mins   Cooking time: 35 mins   Serves: 6-8

Ingredients

4 very large crabs
3 tomatoes, finely chopped
½ cup coriander leaves, finely chopped
Juice of 3 limes
3 sprigs curry leaves
Salt
Peanut or Coconut oil

For the ground masala paste
(Grind fine with water)
14 large Reshampatti chillies, deseeded
2 onions, finely chopped
1 fresh coconut, grated
12 large garlic cloves
2" piece of ginger
2" piece of fresh turmeric or dry 1" piece
1 tbsp broiled, coriander seeds
1 tbsp broiled fennel seeds
3 green cardamom seeds
10 black peppercorns
1" piece cinnamon

Method

1.   Clean and cut the crab as described on pg. 13.

2.   Mix 3 tbsp oil with the ground masala in a vessel. Fry the masala over a low flame till it becomes red. Add the crab pieces and stir for 5 minutes. Add 3 cups water and allow the curry to simmer for 10 minutes. Taste for salt.

3.   Heat 2 tablespoons oil in a large vessel, and splitter the curry leaves. Stir in the tomatoes and chopped coriander and cook well over a low flame. Add the curry to the tomato mix here and bring the gravy to boil. Remove from fire.

4.   Add the lime juice to the curry and stir well.

5.   Serve hot with basmati rice, green chillies cooked in mustard sauce and rice papads.

Bengali Crab Curry
(Kakkrar Jhol)

Preparation time: 15 mins   Cooking time: 35 mins   Serves: 6-8

Ingredients

6 crabs, cleaned and cut into
body and claws.
3 onions, sliced
3 bay leaves
6 potatoes, each cut into 4 wedges
2 sprigs curry leaves
Coarse salt
Mustard oil/Peanut oil/Pure ghee

For the ground masala paste

3 onions
2" ginger
9 green chillies, deseeded and pulped

For the garam masala

1 tbsp turmeric powder
1 tbsp ground cinnamon, peppercorns,
cloves
3 green cardamoms

Method

1.   Cut the crabs if they are very big. Apply salt and turmeric on the pieces.

2.   Take 2 tbsp each of ghee and oil and fry well the crabs and curry leaves till the shell and claws turn red. Remove from fire and keep aside.

3.   Fry the potatoes golden brown in the remaining oil and remove from the pan. Next, fry the ground masala and the garam masala, till an appetizing aroma arises from the vessel. Add the sliced onions and fry them till brown.

4.   Add the sugar and 3 cups of water, the crab and the potato wedges and let the flame simmer for 10 minutes. Taste for salt before removing from the fire.

5.   Serve with white rice, green salad, papads and raw onions.

Ghol Fillet Sandwiches

Preparation time: 12 mins   Cooking time: 20 mins   Serves: 4

Ingredients

8 equal sized ghol fillets, 2½" x 2½"
1 cup fine shrimps, washed and dried
1 spring onion, finely chopped
Salt
Peanut oil
Thin white string

For the ground masala paste

(Grind fine with vinegar)
4 green chillies, deseeded
2 red dried chillies, deseeded
6 large garlic cloves
1 tsp cumin seeds
7 peppercorns
2 tbsps coriander, chopped

Method

1.   Wash the fillets and salt them.

2.   Place the ground masala in a small vessel. Add the shrimps and spring onion and mix well. Apply it thickly on each fillet. Cover with another fillet and tie the pair with a thin string. Repeat with the other pieces.

3.   Heat and fry 2 pairs at a time. Turn over the fish gently and fry till both sides are golden brown.

4.   Serve hot with finger chips and green salad.

Tandoori Ghol Fish Fillets

Preparation time: 15 mins   Cooking time: 40 mins   Serves: 6

Ingredients

12 large 4" fillets of ghol
Juice of 3 sour limes
1 tsp aji-no-moto
1 tbsp black pepper powder
1 tbsp coriander, chopped
Salt
Oil

Method

1.   Apply the fish with a mixture of aji-no-moto, pepper and salt.

2.   Mix the lime juice with an equal amount of peanut oil and apply all over the fillets. Sprinkle with coriander and marinate for 4-6 hours.

3.   Cook over hot coals, basting the fish with extra oil and cook till tender and golden in colour.

4.   Serve hot with hot and spicy tomato sauce (pg. 4).

Fish Fillets with Piquant Orange Sauce

Preparation time: 15 mins   Cooking time: 35-40 mins   Serves: 4-6

Ingredients

For the Fillets

4 large fillets of pomfret or sole or ghol
each cut into 2 pieces
Juice of 2 sour limes
1 tsp black pepper powder
Rock salt
2 eggs
Breadcrumbs
Salt
Butter/Peanut or Sunflower oil

For the sauce

350 gms tomatoes, skinned and pulped
1 cup orange juice
2 small onions, cut in fine slices
5 garlic cloves, minced
2 green chillies, deseeded and finely cut
1 pinch red chilli powder
1 pinch black pepper powder
1 tsp tabasco or capsico sauce

Method

1.   Marinade the fillets and keep aside for 2 hours.

2.   Make the sauce first and fry the fillets last.

3.   To make the sauce put 2 tablespoons of butter and the onion slices and minced garlic and cook over a low flame till soft and pink. Add the tomato pulp and orange juice and cook for 5 minutes. Add the green chillies, the chilli and black pepper powders and the tabasco or capsico sauce. Taste for salt. Allow the sauce to cook for 3 minutes more and remove from the heat.

4.   Place a clean frying pan, half filled with oil on medium heat.

5.   Whisk 2 eggs. Dip the fillets in the egg and coat with the breadcrumbs. Fry in hot oil till crisp and golden.

6.   Serve the fillets hot with warm orange sauce, boiled cauliflower and brocolli florets.

Ghol Cakes with Cheese

Preparation time: 20 mins   Cooking time: 20-25 mins   Serves: 8-12

Ingredients

750 gms boneless ghol,
cut into large pieces

600 gms potatoes, mashed

200 gms mushrooms, finely chopped

250 gms cheese, grated

6 green chillies, deseeded

1" fresh ginger, finely sliced

¼ cup parsley or coriander leaves,
finely chopped

1 tsp black pepper powder

Juice of 3 sour limes

3 tsps sugar

1 tbsp butter

4 eggs

Breadcrumbs

Salt

Peanut or Sunflower oil

Method

1.   Boil the ghol fish after washing it. Add salt and sliced ginger and cook till tender. Drain in a sieve and place in a flat plate. Add the mashed potatoes and mix well with the fish. Add the grated cheese and mix.

2.   Saute the mushrooms in butter and add them to the fish mixture. Add the green chillies, pepper powder and parsley or coriander. Mix the lime juice and sugar through and add to the fish. Taste for salt.

3.   Make round patties, flattened at the top and bottom. Roll in breadcrumbs.

4.   Heat oil in a deep frying pan over a medium flame.

5.   Whip the eggs in a soup plate.

6.   When the oil gets hot, lower the flame a little, and dip each patty into the whisked eggs and deep fry in the hot oil in small batches of 4 to 5 till golden red.

7.   Serve on a bed of finely chopped lettuce, surrounded by slices of sweet lime, beetroot and tomatoes.

Hakh Gadh – Kashmiri Style Fish

Preparation time: 12 mins   Cooking time: 35-40 mins   Serves: 6-8

Ingredients

650 gms any thick white fish fillets, such as ghol, salmon or kingfish, cleaned, cut and washed
450 gms Kashmiri Hakh or Spinach
150 gms onions, finely sliced
2 tsps Kashmiri chilli powder
½ tsp shahjeera seeds
4 green cardamoms, crushed

1 tbsp garlic, creamed
1 tbsp turmeric, powdered
1 tbsp sesame seeds, roasted
1 tbsp flaked almonds
1 pinch sugar
Salt
Pure ghee

Method

1.   Bring a large pan of water to boil and add the spices, such as cardamoms, ½ tsp Kashmiri chilli powder, turmeric powder, creamed garlic and salt.

2.   Cut the spinach fine and add to the aromatic boiling water. Cook till the water has almost dried up. Remove the pan from the fire.

3.   Coat the fish pieces, with salt and remaining Kashmiri chilli powder and fry until golden-brown. Put in the cooked spinach. Roast the shahjeera, sprinkle the seeds on top of the fish pieces. Swirl the vessel gently from time to time while fish cooks.

4.   Fry the onions in ghee and sprinkle over the fish. Cook on a very low fire for 5 minutes and serve immediately.

Kashmiri Mugh Gadh – Fish Cooked with Radish Slices

Preparation time: 12-15 mins   Cooking time: 40-45 mins   Serves: 8-10

Ingredients

900 gms thick white fish fillets of salmon, kingfish or ghol

500 gms thick long white radish, scraped, cut into ¼" slices and then halved

250 gms deep-fried onion paste

10 gms Kashmiri chilli paste

16 gms garlic paste

2 pieces of cinnamon (about 2")

3 cloves

2 whole green cardamoms

3 black cardamoms

1½ tbsps turmeric powder

1½ tsps green cardamoms, powdered

2 tsps black peppercorns, powdered

1 tsp black cumin, powdered

2½ tsps dry ginger powder

Salt

Pure ghee

Method

1. Sprinkle the cut radish with a little coarse salt and set it aside.

2. Cut the fish fillets into 2" squares and salt them.

3. Heat ½ cup ghee in a frying pan and fry the fish until golden brown.

4. Take a large vessel and use the ghee left over from frying the fish. Wash the radish slices and pat them dry. Warm the ghee, sauté the garlic and radish slices until cooked.

5. Heat 1 tbsp ghee in another pan and fry the ground onion and chilly pastes, along with the whole spices. Add the spice powders and toss in the sautéed radish. Add ½ cup water and bring to a boil. Add the fish and simmer till flavours are well blended.

6. Serve hot with rotis and pickle or chutney.

Bengali Fish Pulao

This is an unusual way of cooking the rice very much like the way it is cooked in northern India in the mutton yakhni itself. The fragrance of the pulao is very delicious in an airy, light way. The fish taste does not detract from the delicate fragrance of the rice.

Preparation time: 15 mins   Cooking time: 50 mins   Serves: 6-8

Ingredients

For the Rice:
600 gms basmati rice
2 large onions, coarsely chopped
1 tbsp broiled coriander seeds, crushed
1 tbsp broiled anise seeds, crushed
1 tbsp broiled cumin seeds, crushed
4 green cardamoms, crushed
3 mace flowers, crushed
1½" piece ginger, chopped
1 tbsp pure ghee
Salt

For the Fish:
10 (2½") fillets of rohu, mahseer, ghol, or pomfret
3 sprigs curry leaves
15 large garlic cloves, finely sliced
Mustard oil

For the ground masala
(Grind with ½ cup of water)
6 Kashmiri chillies
1 cup fresh coriander, finely chopped
2 tbsps mint, freshly chopped
1 tbsp anise seeds
1 tbsp turmeric powder
½ tbsp cumin seeds, broiled
Juice of 2 sour limes

For garnishing
2 sliced onions, deep fried and crisp

Method

1.   Wash the rice and keep it aside. Place a large pot on a medium flame with sufficient water to cook the rice. Add 2 cups extra for evaporation whilst boiling. Take all the crushed spices, the raw onion and ginger and tie it all up in a large square

muslin cloth, to place in the water. Tie the four ends together with a long white cord, which should extend from the pot to the table so that you can pull it up easily. Boil the water for 25 minutes at a fast boil. Add the washed rice, salt, and more water if necessary. Cook till fluffy and tender.

2.   Grind all the masala, till soft. Squeeze the lime juice in it and spread the masala all over the salted fish fillets.

3.   Place 3 tablespoons of mustard oil in a frying pan over moderate heat. Allow the oil to smoke, then reduce the heat and add the curry leaves and the sliced garlic. Stir for 2 minutes and fry the fish till crisp in 2 or 3 batches. Place it in a flat plate.

4.   Remove the hot rice onto a salver and dot with pure ghee and place the fried fish pieces on top of the rice. Cover with crisp fried onions.

Accompaniments:

A green salad and sour lime wedges
Spicy egg curry
Chum-chum

Making a Meal out of a Hilsa

The meal would begin with a dish of Chhanchra of Hilsa head, cooked with green leafy vegetables.

After this, Hilsa oil is eaten poured over white rice along with pieces of fried daga.

This will be followed by fried roe portions.

The end of the meal sees a serving of peti/stomach portion cooked in a strong mustard sauce.

Or there may even be a thin jhol of Hilsa cooked with brinjal and potatoes.

Bangladeshi Hilsa Roe

The Bengalis eat this kind of cooked roe with rice. However, it could also be eaten with rotis and frenchbeans cooked in coconut.

Preparation time: 5 mins   Cooking time: 18-20 mins   Serves: 4-5

Ingredients

Large hilsa roe
½ tsp turmeric
5 green chillies, deseeded and pulped
4 green chillies, deseeded and slit
2 medium sized potatoes

2 medium onions, finely chopped
Juice of 2 sour limes
2 tsps sugar
Salt
Mustard oil

Method

1.   Wash the roe twice and separate the 2 parts and place them in a rounded vessel or bowl.

2.   Mash it up with a spoon. Separate the thin membranes which hold the roe and discard them.

3.   Add the chilli paste, turmeric and salt to the crushed roe.

4.   Peel the potatoes and cut them into ¼" cubes. Wash the pieces, mix with the onions, add salt and fry in ½ cup mustard oil in a deep-frying pan.

5.   Fry till the potatoes become soft and brown. Then add the mashed fish roe and the slit green chillies and gently stir the mixture until it becomes brown and is ready to eat.

6.   Add the lime juice and sugar and mix into the roe. Remove the vessel from the fire.

7.   Serve with rice or rotis.

Hilsa Smoked in Banana Leaves

In olden times, this recipe was cooked amidst the hot ashes of a wooden fire.

Preparation time: 15-20 mins   Cooking time: 35 mins   Serves: 5-6

Ingredients

10 large pieces hilsa

3 tbsps ground mustard paste

1" turmeric, ground

3 dried red chillies, ground to a paste

6 green chillies, ground to a paste

Salt

Mustard oil

8 large long pieces of banana leaves

Method

1.   Wash the fish pieces well. Apply salt, turmeric paste, mustard paste and chilli paste. Pour over ½ cup of mustard oil.

2.   Take a large iron tava or griddle. Oil it with a piece of cloth. Spread 4 pieces of leaves in a vertical position and 4 long leaves in a horizontal position like a cross. Place all the fish in the center of the leaves and form into a tight package and tie it with a string.

3.   Heat the tava over a strong flame and cook the banana wrapped package, carefully moving it around the tava for 30 minutes. The banana leaves will sizzle and slowly turn black.

4.   Place the package on a flat dish and remove fish from the leaves.

5.   Serve hot with rice.

Hilsa in Mustard Gravy
(Bengali Shorshe Ilish)

Preparation time: 10 mins   Cooking time: 25 mins   Serves: 4-6

Ingredients

9-10 pieces of hilsa *peti*
1½-2 tbsps of black mustard
1½-2 tbsps of black mustard ground
with 2 deseeded green chillies and a
pinch of coarse salt

8 green chillies, slit and deseeded
Turmeric powder or paste
Salt
Mustard oil

Method

1.   Wash and salt the *peti* pieces.

2.   Rub the fish pieces with the turmeric powder or paste.

3.   Heat 4 to 5 tablespoons of mustard oil in a large vessel. Add the ground mustard paste along with ½ teaspoon of turmeric. Stir for 5 minutes and add 1½ cups of water and bring it to a boil.

4.   Gently add the *peti* pieces and the green chillies. Taste for salt.

5.   Cover the vessel and cook for 10 minutes over a medium heat. Allow the water to evaporate until the fish is covered by a thick, yellow gravy. Remove from the fire.

6.   Serve with rice.

Fried Hilsa/Bhing Roes

Preparation time: 2 Hrs   Cooking time: 20-25 mins   Serves: 10-12

Ingredients

8 hilsa/bhing roes, divided into 2 parts
3 tbsps red chilli powder
2 tbsps turmeric powder
1 tbsp black pepper powder

Juice of 4-6 sour limes
Coarse salt to taste
Til or sesame oil

Method

1.   Very carefully wash the roes and place on a large tray. Separate each roe from the center into two parts. Apply the chilli, turmeric, black pepper powder and salt. Sprinkle the lime juice, turn over and marinate for 2 hours.

2.   Place the roes in hot oil and cover the frying pan with a lid. Lower the heat and cook for 5-7 minutes. Now turn them over and fry without covering. Cut each roe into 4 or 6 pieces, depending on the size of the roe.

3.   Serve hot with slices of sour lime.

Govarsing-ne-gharab-no-patio

This is a traditional recipe of the Parsis who formerly lived in the coastal towns of Gujarat where fish was available in abundance. "Patio" is a thick gravy made with different vegetables, onions, tomatoes and special masalas. Usually the fish is added when the gravy is just about to be done. Govarsing are cluster beans and "gharab" is bhing fish roe.

Preparation time: 45-50 mins   Cooking time: 25-30 mins   Serves: 8

Ingredients

2 pairs fresh bhing roes
500 gms govarsing or cluster beans
1 tsp chilli powder
1 tsp turmeric powder
½ cup thick tamarind pulp
½ cup jaggery
4 large tomatoes, finely chopped
3 large onions
1 sprig curry leaves
½ cup coriander, finely chopped
Salt
Oil for cooking

Grind in ½ cup of vinegar

½ coconut, grated
1 tbsp sesame seeds
1 tbsp cumin seeds
1 tsp black peppercorns
½" piece cinnamon
2 cloves
1 badiyan or star anise
1 whole pod garlic cloves
4 green chillies, deseeded
5 red Kashmiri chillies
1 tsp turmeric powder

Method

1.   Wash the two pairs of fish roes very carefully and separate each of the two parts with a knife. Marinate the fish roe in salt, 1 tsp of turmeric powder and 1 tsp of chilli powder. Set aside in a cool place.

2.   Grind the required masala to a fine paste on a stone mortar with ½ cup of vinegar.

3.   String the cluster beans and cut or break into 3 pieces each. Boil in a pot of salted water and when soft, strain through a colander.

4.   Place the curry sprigs and chopped onions along with 1 cup of oil in a large, thick-bottomed vessel and cook the onions until soft. Add the ground masala, tomatoes, tamarind pulp and jaggery and cook for 10 minutes over a low fire.

5.   Meanwhile, place an iron skillet or non-stick frying pan onto a stove. Add 1 cup oil and deep fry the 4 large pieces of roe and then cut each piece into 4 portions to total 16 pieces. Fry well until golden brown.

6.   To the masala gravy, add the boiled cluster beans and stir. Spread the vegetable evenly in the pot and place the pieces of fish roe on top. Cover the vessel and gently cook over a low fire. After 10 minutes, uncover, turn the roe pieces over and cook for 5 more minutes. Top with the chopped coriander.

7.   Serve with rotis or parathas.

The Lobsters

The Indian lobster is known as the spiny lobster and is slightly different from the true lobsters of other countries because they do not have the huge crushing claws that the others have. Until some years ago, lobsters were looked down upon as food for poor people. Only recently has it come into its own, because of demands for it by foreign markets.

It is found in India, Mauritius, Natal, Sri Lanka, Singapore, Borneo, Java, Japan, Tahiti and the Great Barrier Reef.

Lobster or Crab Stuffed Grapefruit Cocktail

Preparation time: 45 mins - 1hr   Arranging time: 45 mins   Serves: 15

Ingredients

10 grapefruits, each cut into 2 pieces
Boiled crab meat from 14 crabs or lobster meat from 10 lobsters
2 large tins sliced pineapples

1 large tin gherkins
2 large cups mayonnaise
2 tbsps tabasco or capsico sauce
1 cup tomato sauce

Fresh fruits and vegetables for decoration:

4 sweet limes
2 oranges
1 papaya
1 watermelon
1 fresh pineapple
2 bunches green grapes

2 bunches parsley
1 small can cherries
2 tbsps brandy (optional)
1 kg green cabbage, shredded
6 tomatoes
6 spring onions
Salt
Pepper

Method

1.   Assemble the salad mixture and chill it in the refrigerator. Half an hour before eating time, place the grapefruit in a silver salver and start decorating the dish.

2.   Use live crabs and boil them in salted water. Remove all the unnecessary portion and retain only the soft white flesh. Spread and place in the refrigerator.

If using lobsters, retain the head pieces and empty tail shells for use as decoration. Dip the lobsters into salted boiling water and cook till they turn red. Then save the heads and remove the white flesh from the tails.

3.   Cut the grapefruits into two pieces. Cut with a sharp penknife in a saw toothed design. Remove the pulp and make juice in a liquidizer and use as and when required.

4.   Turn the grapefruit shells upside down on a tray and refrigerate.

5.   In a large glass bowl, place the crab or lobster meat. Add salt, freshly ground pepper, tomato sauce and tabasco sauce. Cover with foil and chill.

6.   Cut the gherkins and pineapple slices into small strips and add to the flesh in the bowl. Mix in the mayonnaise sauce. Add the brandy if you are using it. Cover and chill.

7.   Cut the papaya and the watermelon into flower shapes. Do the same with the sweet limes and oranges. Shred the cabbage. Place the cabbage in iced water. Keep a steady hand while cutting the fruit. If necessary, draw the outlines in pencil on the fruit before cutting into it with a sharp penknife. Cut slices from the fresh pineapple.

8.   Place the cabbage on the mirror or salver. Decorate the edges with pineapple slices. Stuff the grapefruit cups with the mixed salad and decorate each with a cherry and tiny parsley sprig. Arrange the cut papaya at one end of the dish and stuff with the green grapes. Place the cut sweet limes in between the grapefruit cups. Place the watermelon at the other end of the dish and decorate the rest of the dish with 6 roses made from the skin of the six tomatoes.

9.   Place the whole salver on another dish full of crushed ice in the centre of the buffet table and serve. One grapefruit for one person and some extra cups for doubles should always be taken into account. If using a mirror, place directly on the table.

10. If desired, decorate the dish or mirror with the lobster head and tails. This is a very delicious item and the only difficulty is the arrangement of the fruits.

11. Fruits can be cut in a variety of ways. You can make a basket out of the watermelon and stuff it with black and green grapes.

Bengali Lobster Curry
(Galda Chingrir)

Preparation time: 20 mins   Cooking time: 20-25 mins   Serves: 4-6

Ingredients

6 large crayfish or lobsters, well cleaned
Milk from 1 freshly grated coconut
2 tbsps ginger-garlic paste
2 tbsps Kashmiri chilli paste
2 onions, chopped fine
4 green chillies, deseeded and chopped fine

4 green cardamoms, lightly crushed
10 black peppercorns, lightly crushed
½" cinnamon piece
5 medium sized potatoes, peeled and cut into 4" pieces each
Pure ghee
Salt

Method

1.   Clean the lobsters well. Discard shells and devein. Wash well, apply salt and turmeric and set aside.

2.   Heat the ghee in a large vessel over a medium flame. When hot, sautée the onions and chillies.

3.   Add the lobsters and the potatoes and mix well for 5 minutes. Add the ground pastes such as ginger-garlic and red chillies, as well as the cardamoms, peppercorns and cinnamon piece. Stir for 5 minutes more and add the coconut milk. Taste for salt.

4.   Lower the heat and allow the lobsters and potatoes to simmer in the coconut milk over a very low fire for 15 minutes till soft and tender.

5.   Serve with ghee rice or vegetable pulao.

Steamed Lobster with Red Chilli Sauce

Preparation time: 7-10 mins   Cooking time: 45 mins   Serves: 4

Ingredients

1 large lobster with shell, cleaned and deveined

Juice of 2 sour limes

2 whole peppercorns

3 celery pieces each 2" long

1 medium onion, finely minced

2 tsps ginger, finely minced

2 tsps garlic, finely minced

3 fresh red chillies, finely ground

2 tsps chilli oil

2 tbsps chilli sauce (ready made)

2 tbsps tomato sauce

¼ cup refined oil

Salt

Method

1.   Wash the lobster and place it in a large pan of boiling water. Add salt, lime juice, peppercorns, minced ginger and celery pieces.

2.   Allow to cook over moderate heat.

3.   When the flesh is tender, drain the water.

4.   In a saucepan sautée the oil with onion, ginger and garlic. Cook, stirring over a medium flame till the onion is pink and soft. Add the ground red chillies, chilli oil and chilli sauce. Keep stirring and allow to come to gentle boil. Add salt to taste, remove from the fire and serve in a separate bowl along with the lobster.

Steamed Lobster with
Red Chilli Sauce ❯

Lobster on Toast

Ingredients

200 gms canned or fresh lobster meat
4 small spring onions, finely chopped
4 green chillies, deseeded and finely chopped
25 gms cheese, grated
½ tsp black pepper powder

Juice of 1 sour lime
Pinch of aji-no-moto
1 whisked egg
4 large slices bread, each cut into 3 strips
Salt
Peanut oil

Method

1.   Flake the lobster flesh in a bowl. Add the onions, chillies, cheese, pepper powder, lime juice, aji-no-moto and a pinch of fine salt. Mix well.

2.   Whisk the egg separately and add to the mixture. Place it in the refrigerator for 20 minutes to solidify.

3.   Place a frying pan half-filled with peanut oil on a medium flame. Meanwhile, apply the lobster mixture to the bread strips.

4.   When the oil is hot, place a few strips at a time in the pan, mixture side down and fry to a golden brown on both sides. Place on paper napkins and serve hot with garlic sauce or tomato ketchup.

◀ *Mackerel in Hot Gravy*
Neer Dosa

Tandoori Lobsters

Preparation time: 45 mins   Cooking time: 40 mins   Serves: 5-7

Ingredients

10 large lobsters
Juice of 2 sour limes
300 gms thick yoghurt
1 tsp aji-no-moto
Salt
Oil

For the ground masala paste

(Grind in ¼ cup sugarcane vinegar)
6 Kashmiri red chillies
2 tbsps garlic paste
1 tbsp black peppercorns
1 tbsp mango powder
1 tsp cloves
1 tsp bits of cinnamon

Method

1.   Trim the whiskers of the lobsters. Turn the lobsters over and, making a sharp cut, devein them. Clean as explained on pg. 12. Wash thrice and apply salt and sprinkle aji-no-moto on the soft surface portions of the lobsters.

2.   Grind the masala and mix it into the yoghurt. Whisk well and apply to the lobsters. Marinate overnight in the refrigerator.

3.   Thaw the lobsters properly. Place on a grid over hot coals and baste with oil to prevent drying. Cook over white-hot coals till tender.

4.   Serve with toasted garlic bread and a green salad.

The Indian Mackerel

The most well-known Indian mackerel is called Rastrelliger Kanagurta. In Hindi, it is called "Bangdi", in Marathi "Bangda", in Kannada also it is called "Bangda".

It is an important fish like the sardine because of its oil. Its catches comprise 15% of all the fish caught in India. About 80% to 90% of mackerel come from the West Coast of India.

Its head is the same as the height of the body. Its eyes are covered with thick eyelids. It has small teeth in a single row.

It is blue-grey in colour and yellow on its stomach and sides.

This fish is found in the Indian and Pacific oceans. It also occurs along the whole of the coastal waters of East Africa, north of the Seychelles, Malagassy, Mauritius and Reunion Islands, countries bordering the Red Sea and the Persian Gulf, Pakistan, India, Andaman and Nicobar Islands, Sri Lanka, Burma, Malaysia, Thailand, Cambodia, Indonesia, Borneo, Northern Australia, New Guinea, Polynesia, Samoa and Fiji Islands, Philippines, China, Hong Kong and Taiwan, as well as Hawaii.

This fish is a surface feeder and its main food is plankton.

Mackerel Cutlets

Preparation time: 15-20 mins   Cooking time: 20-25 mins   Serves: 6-8

Ingredients

10 large mackerels, cleaned, washed with heads chopped off

1 small onion, finely chopped

1/4 cup coriander, finely chopped

10 curry leaves, finely chopped

1/4 tsp mustard seeds

1 large boiled potato, mashed well

Juice of 1 sour lime

2-4 eggs

Breadcrumbs

Salt

Peanut oil

For the ground masala paste

6 large cloves garlic

6-8 green chillies, deseeded

1 tsp broiled cumin seeds

1/4 tsp ajwain seeds

Method

1.   Salt the washed mackerel and boil them in 2 cups of water for 7 minutes. Drain the water and carefully debone the fish. Place the fish in a flat plate.

2.   Place the finely chopped onion, coriander and mashed potato along with the fish. Add the ground masala paste.

3.   Take a small saucepan. Put 1 teaspoon of oil in it and place on a medium flame. When hot, put in the curry leaves and mustard seeds and allow to crackle for 2 minutes. Then pour this over the fish. Also add the lime juice. Mix well until you have a smooth mixture. Taste for salt.

5.   Divide the mixture into 16 balls.

6.   Spread breadcrumbs over a wooden board. Place one ball upon it at a time and with the side of a blunt knife, make it into an oval cutlet. When all the cutlets have been made, heat a large frying pan with oil on a medium flame.

7.   Beat 2 eggs in a soup plate till frothy.

8.   When the oil becomes hot, dip a few cutlets at a time in the eggs and release them into the hot oil and fry till golden brown. Serve with any vegetable or dal.

Mackerels in Hot Gravy

Preparation time: 20 mins   Cooking time: 15-20 mins   Serves: 8

Ingredients

16 large mackerel tails – with the portion above stomach level chopped off

2 large onions, sliced

¼ - ½ cup tamarind pulp

5 triphal, crushed

7 kokam

2 sprigs curry leaves

Salt

Coconut oil

For the ground masala paste

½ fresh coconut, grated

20 Kashmiri chillies, deseeded

4 green chillies, deseeded

1" piece turmeric

2" piece ginger

2 tsps cumin seeds

2 tsps coriander seeds

Method

1. Wash and salt the mackerel tails.

2. Grind the masala very fine. Place the onions in a thick-bottomed vessel and add 3 tablespoons of oil and heat on the stove.

3. When the oil sizzles, add the curry leaves and sautée the onions till pink and soft. Add the masala and mix vigorously for 3 minutes. Add the crushed triphal and the kokum and place on a low heat along with a sprinkling of salt.

4. Arrange the mackerels neatly over the masala and pour the tamarind pulp mixed with 1 cup of water over the mackerel.

5. Shake the pan, holding it with 2 kitchen napkins, until the thick masala comes up on top. Gently turn over the mackerels once. Taste for salt.

6. Remove from the fire once the mackerels are cooked.

7. Serve with dal and roti or plain rice or vegetable khichdi.

Dry Pickled Mackerel with Triphal

Preparation time: 7-9 mins   Cooking time: 20 mins   Serves: 6

Ingredients

10 large dried mackerel tails,
each cut into 3 thin pieces
5 triphal
12 curry leaves
3 split green chillies
Salt
½ cup coconut or peanut oil

For ground masala paste
(Grind fine in ½ cup of tamarind water)
10 Kashmiri chillies
1½ tbsps broiled coriander seeds
1 tbsp broiled cumin seeds
1 tbsp broiled grams (skinned)
1 tbsp broiled peanuts
8 large cloves of garlic
6 black peppercorns

Method

1.   Wash the pieces of fish and salt them carefully. Normally dried fish need no salt.

2.   Take a heavy bottomed vessel and put in the finely ground masala and mix well. Add the triphal, curry leaves, green chillies and mix again. Then pour the oil over the salted fish and mix into the masala.

3.   Place over a low to medium heat and cook without water until the fish is done.

The Molluscs

Molluscs occur in the shallow coastal regions of India, in estuaries and brackish water habitats.

Mussels, scallops, oysters, clams and other bi-valve molluscs such as abalones, snails, univalves and squids, cuttlefish, octopi, and nautilus have been used by man from very ancient times. Pearls from the pearl oyster are highly prized. Their thick lustrous, iridescent shells called "mother-of-pearl" are in great demand.

The **sea mussels** are found attached by means of anchoring byssus threads to coastal rocks and other hard rocks covered by the tides. They are found in very shallow water receding to 15 metre depths. The mussel beds often extend into estuaries and brackish water areas where the salinities are about the same as sea water. In India, we have 2 varieties, the green mussel and the brown mussel.

Mussels feed on detritus, diatoms and microplankton.

Edible oysters are found in temperate and tropical waters, on hard rocky or semi-hard sandy substrata. They are also found in bays and creeks, estuaries and brackish water zones. Several generations of them are set close upon each other so that they form reefs close to tidal ranges. They are cemented firmly to the substratum by one of their shell valves.

In many countries outside India, oysters are greatly relished and being expensive, can be afforded only by rich people. Because of the great demand for them, they are **cultured** on an industrial rearing and harvested. This culturing sees that a steady supply of clean, well shaped, hygienically pure shell fish is available for human consumption.

Oysters are very nutritious and are rich in vitamins A and B. They contain adequate quantities of glycogen, protein and other health giving minerals. They also have an excellent flavour.

In India, we do not have a large scale production of oysters. You find them in high class restaurants. They are sold in a few markets in Bombay.

Clams and Allied Bivalves

These are free living molluscs living on surf-beaten sandy shores or muddy bottoms of bays, estuaries and brackish water zones, including marshy lagoons along both the East and West coasts of India. Most species live in dense beds and are of greater abundance along the West Coast regions. There are many species under different families.

Of Mussels and Clams and Scallops

My very dear friend Rodolphe Van Lancker runs a fish restaurant in Brussels, Belgium. His restaurant is called LEON. Brussels is known as the capital of mussels and fries. Over the years it has become a famous place. It has existed since the past 110 years and 5 generations. It has welcomed famous personalities in the cultural, political and financial world. His clients include the American President Jimmy Carter, Catherine Deneuve as well as members of the Royal Family.

The restaurant has 14 special recipes on mussel alone. Lobster, fish and meat are also available. But, the true gourmet always comes back without fail for the "Moule Speciale" – a secret recipe of mussels, cooked in a casserole accompanied with fries and sprinkled with Belgian Beer.

Since the restaurant was a thumping success, they decided to take the Concept Leon to the International Level.

Within the last 10 years, over 45 restaurants opened in France alone, serving annually 300,000 customers and these consumed 4,380,000 kilos of mussels which is more than 1% of the total world production of mussels.

Eight restaurants were opened in Belgium. Leon de Bruxelles covers 11 buildings. This high spot of Belgian cuisine enjoys an unique success in Belgium.

My friend has even opened a restaurant in Beirut!

Scallops with Garlic Butter Sauce

Preparation time: 10 mins   Cooking time: 40-45 mins   Serves: 6

Ingredients

1 kg shelled scallops, washed
and cut into ¼" slices
150 gms Garlic Butter (recipe on pg. 8)
Flour or self-raising flour
3 tbsps refined vegetable oil

White pepper powder
1 bunch parsley
Few lime slices

Method

1.   Wash the scallops well. Allow to drain in a colander. Sprinkle them with salt and white pepper powder according to taste.

2.   Sprinkle with flour and then shake them so only a light dusting of the flour remains.

3.   Melt butter in a non-stick frying pan over medium heat. Allow the foam to subside and sauté the scallops in batches. Shake the frying pan and stir the scallops so they do not stick to the bottom of the pan.

4.   Once the scallops are lightly browned, place them onto a pyrex dish.

5.   Warm the garlic butter and pour over the scallops and serve immediately.

6.   Decorate with the parsley sprigs and lime slices.

Scallops cooked with Garlic and Cognac

Preparation time: 15-20 mins   Cooking time: 20-25 mins   Serves: 4

Ingredients

16 large scallops, with corals (if possible)   2 tbsps Cognac
8 cloves garlic, finely chopped   Salt
½ cup parsley, chopped   Olive oil
1 tsp black pepper, freshly grated
2 tbsps flour

Method

1.   Clean the scallops. Slice the white flesh into 2 parts. Leave the coral whole. Season the scallop with salt and pepper.

2.   Heat ½ cup olive oil in a large frying pan. Add the chopped garlic and allow to sizzle. Then add the white portion of the scallops. Cook stirring well for 2 minutes only.

3.   Add the corals and cook for 2 more minutes. Add the cognac and within a minute, take the pan off the fire. Sprinkle the parsley over the scallops.

4.   Serve in the scallop shells or on hot toast.

Baked Scallops, Indian Style

Scallops can be baked in large natural shells or in a pyrex dish. You have to prepare the scallops by removing the parts which are inedible (see pg. 12).

Preparation time: 12-15 mins   Cooking time: 25-30 mins   Serves: 4

Ingredients

16 scallops, cleaned, washed and sliced
5 spring onions, 6" long from
root to green leaves
2 green chillies, deseeded
and finely chopped
4 large garlic cloves, ground to a paste
1 tbsp celery, finely chopped
1 tbsp parsley, finely chopped

1 egg
¾ cup milk
½ cup cream
¾ cup butter
¼ cup flour
½ cup cheddar cheese, grated
Salt

Method

1.   Lightly salt the sliced scallops.

2.   Place 2 tablespoons of butter in a large non-stick frying pan on medium heat. When it gets hot, add the garlic, chillies and spring onions and cook lightly over a low flame. Do not allow the onions or garlic to brown. Then add the scallops and fry them for 5 minutes in the mixture and allow to soften. Add ½ cup of hot water and allow to cook till scallops become soft and very little water remains. Remove from the fire.

3.   Place ½ cup of butter in a large saucepan on a low fire. Add the flour and stir till it becomes ivory coloured. Add any water remaining in the cooked scallops and the milk and make a thick white sauce. Taste for salt. Cool. Mix in the cream.

4.   Whisk the egg and mix it into the white sauce. Mix in the cooked scallops. Divide the mixture between the 4 shells.

5.   Sprinkle the cheese over the creamed scallops and bake in a hot oven at 350°F.

6.   Serve with a fruit salad and French bread or crisp bread.

Spanish Shellfish Salad

Preparation time: 30 mins   Cooking time: 30 mins   Serves: 4-6

Ingredients

350 gms each clams and mussels

450 gms large prawns

4 baby gherkins

1 large red pepper, washed and chopped fine

1 green chilli, deseeded and chopped fine

1 medium brown onion, chopped fine

1 tsp black pepper powder

1 tbsp braised whole coriander seeds

½ cup wine vinegar or 2 tbsps sugarcane vinegar

½ cup fresh parsley, chopped

Juice of 1 sour lime

Salt

Olive oil

Method

1.   Clean and wash the mussels and clams. Then boil them in 1 ½ cup water. Remove the flesh from the shells. Discard any unopened clams and mussels.

2.   Shell and de-vein the prawns. Wash thoroughly twice. Marinate in salt, pepper powder and the juice of 1 sour lime and cook very gently for ½ an hour in a non-stick pan till tender.

3.   Beat ½ cup of oil with the vinegar for 10 minutes until thoroughly assimilated. Place all the fish in a pyrex bowl. Mix in the red peppers, chilli, gherkins, onion and parsley. Pour the oil and vinegar over the fish and stir gently till fish is well coated.

4.   Cover the bowl and chill overnight and serve at lunch the next day.

Soupe Aux Moules
(Mussel Soup)

Preparation time: 20 mins   Cooking time: 45-50 mins   Serves: 6

Ingredients

2 kg fresh mussels

500 gms large red tomatoes, pulped

8 cloves crushed garlic

2 medium onions, finely chopped

½ gm saffron strands

½ cup vermicelli

Juice of 2 sour limes

Pepper, fresh grated

Sprigs of fresh basil, thyme, parsley

Salt

Olive oil

Method

1.   Wash the mussels well and place them in a large pot along with 2 litres of water and the herbs. Boil over a high heat for 5 minutes until the mussels open up.

2.   Place mussels in a separate vessel and retain the cooking water.

3.   Put ¼ cup olive oil in a large pot on a medium flame. Add the onion and garlic and cook for 7 minutes then add the pulped tomatoes. Strain the water in which the mussels were boiled through a fine sieve or piece of cloth and add to the tomatoes. Allow to boil.

4.   Heat the saffron on an iron griddle and crumble it into the tomato mixture. Add the vermicelli and salt and pepper. Simmer over a low fire till vermicelli is soft and tender.

5.   Remove the mussels from their shells and add to the gravy. Discard the unopened ones.

6.   Add the lime juice, mix and serve immediately.

Dried Mussels – Saraswat Style

Preparation time: 20 mins   Cooking time: 35-40 mins   Serves: 6

Ingredients

50 shelled mussels
3 onions
½ large fresh coconut, grated
1 tbsp braised coriander leaves
½ tsp asafoetida
¼ cup thick tamarind pulp
3 split green chillies
Salt
Refined oil

For ground masala paste
(Grind fine in a little water)
8 Kashmiri chillies
1" piece ginger
1½ tsp black pepper corns
2 cloves of garlic

Method

1. Cut each onion into half and slice into half moons. Crush the onions with your hand.

2. Place half a cup of oil in a vessel. Put in onions and grated coconut and cook over a medium flame till soft.

3. Add the ground masala and stir well for 5 minutes. Add the mussels and 1 cup water. Cover and cook till mussels are soft and tender.

4. Add the asafoetida and the tamarind pulp. Stir and cook for further 5 minutes.

5. Serve with rice or rotis.

Karwari Mussel Curry

The mussels are shelled and one shell of each is kept back to be used whilst cooking the curry. That is why this curry is also called Ekshipi (meaning one shell) Karwari Curry.

Preparation time: 15-18 mins   Cooking time: 25-30 mins   Serves: 6-8

Ingredients

70 shelled mussels – 35 shells
3 onions, chopped fine
½ cup coriander, finely chopped
8-10 red Kashmiri chillies
2" fresh ginger
7 black peppercorns

2" piece fresh turmeric
1 tbsp braised coriander seeds
½ large coconut, grated
¼ cup tamarind pulp
Salt
Refined oil

Method

1.   In 1 teaspoon of oil, over a hot tawa, roast the chillies, black peppercorns, coriander seeds, turmeric, ginger and grated coconut without burning or charring.

2.   Grind the roasted masala, along with 1 finely chopped onion to a fine paste.

3.   Heat ½ cup of oil in a large vessel on medium heat. Add the onions and cook till pink. When onions are soft, add the ground masala and fry for 3 minutes and then add the washed mussels and the shells. Allow to simmer after adding 2 to 3 cups of water until the mussels are soft. Then add the tamarind and cook for 7 minutes.

4.   Serve with rice.

Moroccan Samak Charmoula
(Marinated and Baked Mullet)

Mullets are a favourite fish of the Mediterranean people. This Moroccan dish is very popular and you can spice the marinade in different ways.

Preparation time: 20 mins   Cooking time: 1 hour   Serves: 6

Ingredients

1 large silver grey mullet
(approx. 1½ kg)
4 tbsps coriander, chopped
4 tbsps parsley, chopped
1 tbsp red chilli powder
1 tsp black pepper powder

1 tbsp cumin powder
Juice of 2 to 3 sour limes
8-10 large cloves
4-6 green chillies, ground into a paste
Salt
½ cup olive oil

Method

1.   Crush the garlic with 1 tsp of salt in a mortar with a pestle with all the other spices and slowly pour in a thin stream of olive oil. The ingredients should be thoroughly assimilated.

2.   Pour the sauce into a pan and gently warm it over low heat for 2 minutes. Take down from the fire and allow to cool.

3.   Scale and gut the fish from the stomach side. Remove the gills and wash well twice. Make diagonal slashes 4 on each side of the fish. Lightly salt it. Place it in a clay dish or a pyrex dish and pour the sauce over the fish. Cover and chill overnight in the refrigerator.

4.   Next day, when needed, remove the fish 30 minutes before baking. Cover the dish with foil and bake in the oven at 350°F for 50-55 minutes.

5.   Serve with toasted bread, butter and green salad.

Top right: Raw Clams with Hot Tomato Sauce
Top left: Boiled Squid Rings
Below: Steamed Oysters with Mustard Sauce ▶

Red Mullet French-style

Preparation time: 10 mins   Cooking time: 20 mins   Serves: 4-6

Ingredients

4 whole red or any other mullets
30 gms butter
1¼ cups tomato sauce
1 red or golden pepper, deseeded and
cut into tiny squares
1 tbsp red wine
15 stoned black olives
2 tbsps parsley, fresh chopped

1 pinch sage
1 pinch thyme
Black pepper powder
Salt

For garnishing

Sweet lime slices
Lettuce leaves

Method

1.   Wash the mullets well. Season with salt and black pepper powder and coat with melted butter.

2.   Arrange neatly in a pyrex dish.

3.   Mix the tomato sauce, chopped red pepper, sage, thyme and parsley and pour it over the mullets. Then arrange the stoned black olives as you wish.

4.   Bake for 20 minutes or a little more at 350°F.

5.   Decorate with slices of sweet lime and lettuce leaves.

❮ Top: Raw Squid
Below: Squid Rings Fried
in Batter

Fried Masala Oysters

Preparation time: 10 mins   Cooking time: 20 mins   Serves: 4

Ingredients

20 large oysters removed from shells
1 tsp garam masala
1 tsp turmeric powder
1 tsp chilli powder
1 tsp sambhar powder
4 green chillies, deseeded

½ cup coriander, finely chopped
Rice flour
Salt
Oil

Method

1. Wash the oysters thoroughly. Then apply salt and all the spices to them.

2. Place ½ cup oil in a deep frying pan on medium flame.

3. Spread rice flour on a wooden board. Roll each oyster in the flour and dip into hot oil. Fry till plump and golden.

4. Serve at breakfast, tea time or with drinks in the evening.

Oyster Curry with Potatoes and Raw Mangoes

Preparation time: 20 mins   Cooking time: 30-35 mins   Serves: 6

Ingredients

2 doz. large oysters, washed well and salted

3 potatoes, peeled and each cut into 4 pieces and boiled

Milk from ½ coconut

2 tender raw mangoes, skinned and cooked in salted water

2 sprigs curry leaves

¼ cup coriander leaves, chopped

Coarse salt

Peanut oil

For the ground masala paste

½ coconut, grated

2 green chillies, deseeded

8 Kashmiri chillies

1 tbsp broiled coriander seeds

1 small onion, chopped

1" piece ginger

10 peppercorns

½" fresh or dry turmeric piece

Method

1.   Heat the curry leaves in 3 tablespoons of oil in a large vessel placed on medium heat.

2.   When hot, add the ground masala and fry till red. Add the oysters and lower the heat and allow them to cook in their own juice for 3 minutes. Then add 2 cups of water and allow the oysters to simmer for 12 minutes in the curry until they are tender.

3.   Add the boiled potatoes and taste for salt.

4.   Add the boiled mango pieces and the coconut milk. Check again for salt. Allow the curry to simmer for 10 minutes. Remove from the heat.

5.   Serve with rice, onion salad and papads.

Greek Style Octopus in Red Wine

Preparation time: ½ hour   Cooking time: 2¼ hours   Serves: 4-6

Ingredients

1 kg baby octopus, cleaned and washed, eyes, head and beak removed

500 gms onions, halved and sliced into half moons

500 gms ripe tomatoes skinned

6 spring onions, 6" from root to green leaves, finely chopped

6 green chillies, deseeded and finely chopped

4 bay leaves

¼ cup parsley, finely chopped

1 tbsp oregano, chopped

8 large garlic cloves skinned, crushed

1 tbsp sugar

1 cup red wine

¼ cup wine vinegar (if available) or

2 tbsps sugarcane vinegar

Salt

Pepper

Olive oil

Method

1.   Place the washed octopus in a saucepan of boiling water along with ⅓ of the onions, bay leaves and salt. Allow to cook for 1¼ to 2 hours till soft.

2.   Cut an X at the bottom of each tomato. Plunge in boiling water for 2 minutes. Skin and chop finely and set aside.

3.   Drain the octopus from the water and cut into 1" pieces.

4.   Heat 3 tbsps oil in a large saucepan. Add the onions, green chillies and garlic and stir for 5 minutes. Then add the boiled octopus pieces. Cook for 5 more minutes and add the finely chopped tomatoes, oregano, parsley, wine and vinegar and cook over a low fire for 1 hour stirring every now and then till the octopus is soft and pulpy. Taste for salt.

5.   Serve topped with parsley leaves.

Grilled or Tandoori Octopus

Just as we in India dry our Bombay Ducks on lines so do the Greeks hang up the octopus to dry in the hot sun for at least 5 days.

Preparation time: 20 mins   Cooking time: 1½ hrs.   Serves: 6-8

Ingredients

1 kg large octopus, slightly dried
½ bottle white wine
4 sprigs fresh oregano
2 sprigs fresh rosemary

¼ cup chilli-garlic paste
Juice of 3 limes
Salt
Olive oil

Method

1.   Remove the eyes, head and beak of the octopus. Leave the rest whole.

2.   Place the well-washed octopus in a large pan and cover with the white wine and some water. Simmer over a medium flame and allow to boil for 1¼ hours until soft and tender. Drain.

3.   Cut the octopus into 1" pieces and smear the pieces with the chilli and garlic paste and salt. Cover with fresh herbs and pour the lime juice over the pieces. Mix well and chill in the refrigerator overnight.

4.   Next day, when needed, place the pieces on thin tandoori "seeks" and roast over red hot coals upon a tandoori sigri. Brush with left-over marinade.

The Pomfret

The pomfrets are the most popular of all fish eaten in India. The Parsis who live on the West Coast of India would not dream of a wedding feast without fried pomfret, or pomfret in a sweet and sour sauce or pomfret covered in chutney and wrapped in banana leaves and then steamed. They are the most highly priced fish and are found along India's East and West Coasts near Gujarat, Maharashtra, Andhra, Kerala, Tamilnadu and Orissa. Outside India, they are found in the Persian Gulf, the Malayan Archipelago, Pakistan, Hong Kong, China, the Philippines and Indonesia.

There are three types of pomfrets:-

1.   Pampus argenteus or silver pomfret called Saranga or Pamplet in Marathi.

2.   Pampus Chinensis or Chinese Pomfret called Khalwed Kapri-Saranga in Marathi.

3.   Apolectis niger or Black Pomfret called Halwa in Marathi.

The Pomfrets are flat fish, diamond in shape with spines in front of dorsal and anal fins. The lower jaw protrudes a little whilst the gill opening is a vertical slit. Its upper surface is gray, but its head and sides are silvery. The abdomen is white.

The large pomfret reaches a maximum of 18 inches and weighs 8 lbs. As a rule, pomfrets prefer sandy bottoms and feed on small crustaceans, especially prawns and sand fleas. Pomfrets are warm water fishes. Cold spells can kill them; so they migrate to avoid cold.

Off the Florida reefs in the USA, one gets the great Pompano which is 3 feet long and weighs upto 30 pounds.

Pomfret Fillet Sandwiches with Lime and Chilli Sauce

Preparation time: 25 mins   Cooking time: 35 mins   Serves: 6-8

Ingredients

16 large pomfret fillets, washed and salted

2 tbsps parsley, washed and chopped

6 spring onions, 4" from root
to green leaves

6 green chillies, deseeded & finely chopped

8 large garlic cloves, finely chopped

1" ginger, finely chopped

1 tsp black pepper, coarsely ground

1 cup crushed baby shrimps, shelled, washed and deveined

Juice of 1 sour lime

1 tsp sugar

4-5 eggs

Breadcrumbs

Salt

Oil

Method

1.   Mix all ingredients in a bowl except the fillets, lime juice and sugar. Add salt.

2.   Heat 2 tbsps of oil in a non-stick frying pan. Add the fish mixture to it and mix vigorously for 3 minutes. Taste for salt. Lower the flame, cover the pan and keep covered till the fish mixture is cooked. Then mix in the lime juice and sugar and remove from the fire.

3.   Place one fillet on a wooden board. Spread a tablespoon of fish mixture over it. Cover with another fillet, press it down and join the two together.

4.   Make long strings with the leaves of spring onions. Tie the fillets tightly with them in two places to make 8 sets of fillet sandwiches.

5.   Crack the eggs in a soup plate and whisk well. Spread the breadcrumbs on a wooden board and gently coat both sides of the fillets.

6.   Dip the fillets·in egg and deep fry in oil till golden brown. The fillets, being thick will need time to cook properly. Do not overheat the oil. Fry over gentle heat.

7.   Serve the fillet sandwiches with lime and chilli sauce (recipe on pg. 6) and mashed potatoes or fried chips.

Pomfret Slices with Buttered Mushrooms

Preparation time: 15 mins   Cooking time: 15 mins   Serves: 4

Ingredients

8 slices pomfret fish
1 packet fresh mushrooms
Juice of 2 sour limes

2 tsps ground pepper
Salt
Butter

Method

1.   Marinade the fish in salt, lime juice and pepper.

2.   Place 2 tablespoons of butter in a frying pan and add washed, sliced mushrooms. Stir till mushrooms are cooked. Remove from the pan and set aside.

3.   Add more butter to the same pan and fry the fish in 2 batches. When cooked, remove to a flat dish. Reheat mushrooms and place over the fried fish.

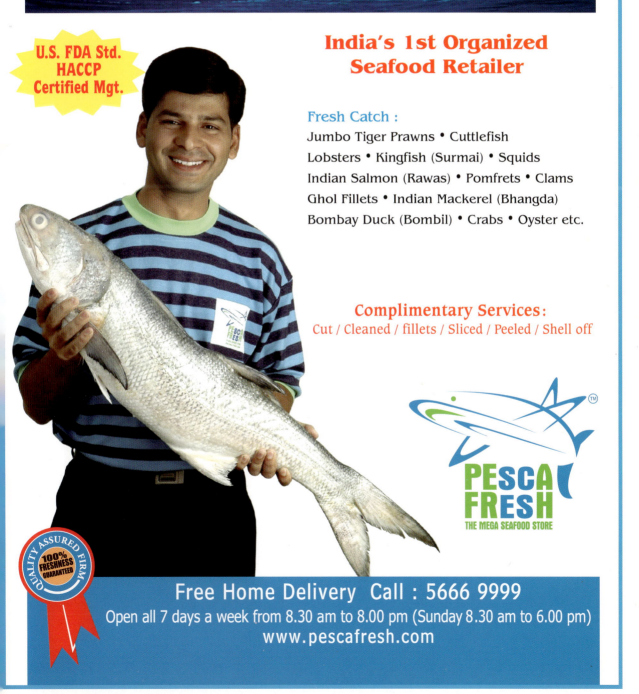

What Mumbai says?

Mid-day
Mumbai based Ace Seafood Bazaar has started what is probably Mumbai's First phone based fresh seafood megastore under the Pesca Fresh brand... Nov 24, 2004.

Bombay Times (downtown plus)
For seafood aficionados in downtown, Pesca Fresh offers a wide range of premium seafood like cuttle fish, clams, oysters squid...their mantra 'from shore to door' ensures that their products are of superior quality and 100% fresh... Jan 14, 2005.

Savvy
With Pesca Fresh, which promises international standard quality control, you don't have to worry on both count, plus they'll send it to you cleaned, cut and neatly packed in temperature controlled containers... April, 2005.

Rashmi Uday Singh-Bombay Times (Times of India)
Don't care to make trips to the fish market, but love fish and want export quality seafood, hygienically processed to FDA standards. ...just call Pesca Fresh.....Sangram Sawant an SGS approved HACCP certified technician is ensuring hygenicaly processed home delivered seafood. Rawas to lobsters and more.... June1st, 2005.

Jame-Jamshed
With the advent of Pesca Fresh, seafood lovers will now discover a world of fresh seafood delicacies. The mantra of 'shore to door' ensures that the seafood lovers need not make a trip to the fish markets.....the seafood is cut, cleaned, fillet....and customized as desired. Accurate weights.....the quality at Pesca Fresh is 100 % guaranteed and consistent...... April 24th, 2005.

Time Out magazine-Mumbai
Try Pesca Fresh who will deliver fresh seafood......in super clean polystyrene. More than a fish monger, Pesca invites their customers to join Club Pesca-a free membership entitles you to monthly newsletters of recipes, health tips, seafood trivia... plus free cookery events and discounts......May 20-June, 2005.

Indian Express
No frozen fish here, each days fresh catch....brought in twice daily...They even clean or fillet the fish on request .Left over fish aren't used for the next days business...... September 20th, 2005.

DNA
Pesca Fresh is a great option for ordering seafood home...they deliver seafood cut and cleaned the way you want.... October 23rd, 2005.

And more.....

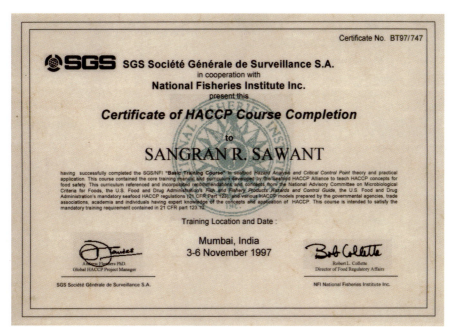

HACCP Certified Management

What is HACCP?

HACCP stands for Hazard Analysis and critical control points which is an industry wide effort initiated by the United States Food and Drug administration originally meant for packaging food for the NASA astronauts. This system is approved by the scientific committee as well as regulatory and industry practitioners. It focuses on best processing practices, optimum hygiene and a system with the motto being, "Prevention is better than cure".

Pesca Fresh and HACCP

The management team at Pesca Fresh has worked in the most sophisticated US markets, has undergone rigorous training and has been certified by SGS societe generale de surveillance, S.A. in cooperation with National Fisheries Institute Inc (USA).

It is with the same ethos of the HACCP system that we hygienically process and supply to our esteemed customers a wide variety of 100 % fresh exotic, fully customized range of seafood to your doorstep.

Pesca Fresh Product List

Grade	Sr. No.	Product	Size
Rawas	1	Indian Salmon / Rawas Whole	800 gms - 1.2 Kg
	2	Indian Salmon / Rawas Large Steaks	51 gms-200gms per pc
Surmai	3	KingFish / Surmai Whole	750 gms - 1.25 Kg
	4	KingFish / Surmai Larg Steak	50-200 gms per pc
Prawns	5	Pesca Super Jumbo Tiger	Under 10 pcs per kg
	6	Jumbo Tiger	11-15 pcs per kg
	7	Premium Large Prawns	15-25 pcs per kg
	8	Large Prawns	25-35 pcs per kg
	9	Premium Medium Prawns	36-45 pcs per kg
	10	Medium Prawns	46-60 pcs per kg
	11	Peeled Prawns	300-500 pcs per kg
Crabs	12	Crabs Medium	200-300 gms per pc
	13	Crabs Large	300-500 gms per pc
	14	Crabs Premium	500gms Up
	15	Crab Meat	Min. 0.5 Kg
Lobsters	16	Medium Lobsters	200-300 gms & up per pc
	17	Large Rock Lobsters	300-500 gms & up per pc
	18	Premium Jumbo Rock Lobster	500 gms & up per pc
Pomfrets	19	White Pomfrets Regular	200-300 gms per pc
	20	White Pomfrets Medium	300-400 gms per pc
	21	White Pomfrets Large	400-500 gms per pc
	22	White Pomfrets Super Xtra Large	500 Up
Chinese Pom	23	Chinese Pomfrets Premium	500 gms & up per pc
Halwa	24	Black Pomfrets/ Halwa Premium	500 gms & up per pc
Mackerels	25	Indian Mackerel / Bhangda Premium	5-8 pcs per kg
	26	Indian Mackerel / Large	8-12 pcs per kg
Bombil	27	Bombay Duck / Bombil	Assorted 12 pcs per kg
Squid	28	Squid Whole U / 10Pc	8 / 20 Pcs.
Ekru	29	Ekru / Grouper	1 Up
Ghols	30	Ghol Whole	1 Up
	31	Ghol Fillets	Fillets
	32	Ghol Steak	50 - 200 gms
Snapper	33	Red Snapper	1Kg up
Lady Fish	34	Lady Fish	100 gms - 250 gms
Sardines	35	Sardines	Assorted
Ribbon Fish	37	Ribbon Fish	200 gms - 400 gms
Rohu	38	Rohu / Betky	1 - 2 Kg
Daara	39	Daara	1000 gms per pc
Clams	40	Clams	100-150 pcs / per kg
Oysters	41	Oysters (Minimum Qty. ½ Doz.)	1 Dozen
Mussels	42	Mussels (Minimum Qty. ½ Doz.)	1 Dozen
PescaJewel	43	Pesca Gift Hamper (Value for Money)	Assorted 5 Varieties

Call : 5666 9999

Free Home Delivery
www.pescafresh.com

Fried Pomfret stuffed with Green Chutney

Preparation time: 35-40 mins   Cooking time: 40 mins   Serves: 6

Ingredients

6 small sized whole pomfrets
1 tbsp turmeric powder
2 tbsps chilli powder
Salt
Oil

For the Chutney

1 portion hot green chutney (see recipe on pg. 10)

Method

1.   Wash the pomfrets. Keep whole. Slit the side of the face and remove the intestines and gills. Wash thoroughly. Apply salt, turmeric and chilli powder to the pomfrets outside and inside. Stuff the stomach through the gills, with as much chutney as possible.

2.   If necessary, tie the pomfret mouths with string so the chutney does not ooze out whilst frying.

3.   Place a large tava or skillet on the stove and cover the bottom with at least ½" of oil. When the oil is hot, place the whole pomfret head first in the oil by the tail. Take a spoon and pour hot oil over the pomfret. When the pomfrets are well fried on both sides, serve with sour lime pieces.

Fish in Banana Leaves

Preparation time: 25 mins   Cooking time: 15 mins   Serves: 6-8

Ingredients

2 large pomfrets 500 gms each, cut into
5 slices each
6 large very soft banana leaves
½ cup vinegar
½ cup water
Salt
½ cup oil

For the Chutney

1 portion hot green chutney (see recipe on pg. 10)

Method

1.   Wash the promfrets twice, apply salt and set aside.

2.   Prepare the banana leaves by removing the center stalk. You will have 12 pieces now. Take 1 slice of fish at a time and smother it in the chutney. It should be well coated and then wrap it in 1 piece of banana leaf into a neat package. Tie with thin white thread. When all the slices are neatly packed, take an aluminium tray and grease it with ½ cup of oil. Place on a medium flame and arrange the packages on the hot tray. Leave for 3 minutes, then turn over once. Sprinkle with water and vinegar and cover tightly. Allow to cook over a low flame for 15 minutes, turning over the packages at least once. Serve immediately.

Greek Psari Ksithato or Cold Fish Fillets

Preparation time: 25 mins   Cooking time: 30 mins   Serves: 6-8

Ingredients

3 pomfrets, each cut into 4 fillets,
i.e. 12 fillets each cut vertically into 2
i.e. 24 long fillets
4 small red onions, sliced into rings
(Grind coarsely)
6 Kashmiri chillies, deseeded
12 large cloves garlic
1 tbsp broiled coriander seeds
1 tbsp broiled sesame seeds

1 kg tomatoes, skinned and chopped
1 tsp turmeric powder
1 tsp black pepper powder
½ cup raisins, washed
½ cup coriander, chopped
1 cup white wine (optional)
Salt
Olive oil

Method

1.   Wash the fillets twice and salt them.

2.   Place half the onion rings in a large frying pan along with half a cup of olive oil. Heat over a medium flame until the onions become pink and translucent. Then place half the fillets in line onto the onion rings. Cook for 4 minutes. Then overturn them and cook for a further 4 minutes. Check that the fish has cooked. Remove from the frying pan and cook the remaining half of the fillets in the same way.

3.   Place the cooked fillets neatly into a large rectangular pyrex dish and allow to cool.

4.   Place the remaining frying pan oil into a saucepan on medium heat. Add the chopped tomatoes and stir lightly. Add 2 teaspoons of sugar to the tomatoes along with the coarsely ground spices. Mix the tomato mixture gently until cooked. Add the wine and cook for a further 5 minutes and then remove from the heat and cool.

5.   Top the cold fillets with the cooled tomato mixture, cover with foil and chill overnight.

6.   Serve the fillets next day with lettuce and cucumber salad and buttered toast.

Crumb Fried Cheese Fish Fillets with Hot Tomato Sauce

Preparation time: 20 mins   Cooking time: 35 mins   Serves: 4-6

Ingredients

1 kg ripe tomatoes, skinned, deseeded, pureed

2 large pomfrets, filleted

Juice of 2 sour limes

2 tsps black pepper powder

2 cups cheese, grated

1 bunch parsley

2 beetroots boiled, sliced

2 lettuce washed

2 cucumbers, skinned and sliced

2 cups toasted breadcrumbs

1 onion sliced

4 eggs, whisked

1 tbsp freshly chopped mint

1 tsp cornflour

Salt

Oil

Method

1.   Wash the fillets and marinate in salt, lime juice and black pepper powder.

2.   Whisk eggs well along with the cornflour in a soup plate.

3.   Heat 4 cups of oil in a large frying pan.

4.   Roll the grated cheese on the inner side of the fish. Dip the fillets in the egg mixture and coat with breadcrumbs and deep fry 3-4 at a time, according to the size of the pan. Remove from the oil when golden brown. Tie 3 sprigs of parsley in bunches and also deep fry.

5.   Arrange the fish fillets and fried parsley on a flat dish covered with lettuce and surrounded by rings of onions, cucumber, beetroot and lemon wedges.

6.   For Hot Tomato Sauce, see recipe on pg. 4.

7.   Serve with the fillets.

Frilled Fillets with Tartare Sauce

Preparation time: 30-45 mins   Cooking time: 20-25 mins   Serves: 4-6

Ingredients
For the Fillets
2 large pomfrets, each cut into fillets
Juice of 2 sour limes
1 tsp black pepper powder
1 tsp red chilli powder
½ cup toasted sesame seeds,
coarsely crushed
2-3 cups toasted breadcrumbs
6 eggs whisked
1 tbsp cornflour
Salt
Oil

For Tartare Sauce
See recipe on pg. 4.

For Garnishing
1 sliced fresh pineapple – with skin.
Diagonally chopped spring onions,
carrots julienne and tomato wedges.

Method

1.   Wash the fillets. Marinate for ½ an hour in salt, chilli powder, pepper and lime juice.

2.   Whisk the eggs in a bowl along with the cornflour.

3.   Mix the breadcrumbs and sesame seeds. Heat oil in a large frying pan. When the oil starts smoking, lower the heat a little and roll the fillets in the breadcrumbs and sesame seeds. Dip in the egg and deep fry 2-3 fillets at a time. If the oil is scorching, the fillets will become dark coloured. So adjust heat as needed.

4.   Lay a dark green banana leaf on a silver salver and stack the fillets neatly in the centre. Surround with pineapple slices. Scatter the carrots and spring onions over the fish. Alternately you can serve it with tomato wedges or sliced papayas.

5.   Serve with the chilled tartare sauce.

Fish Fillets Chilled and Served with Prawn Mayonnaise

Preparation time: 35 mins   Cooking time: 20 mins   Serves: 6-8

Ingredients

1 iceberg lettuce
1 sliced orange
8 fillets of salmon or pomfrets,
2" long x ½" thick
1 cup mayonnaise
1 cup boiled, salted prawns
2 tbsps parsley, chopped
1 tsp garlic, minced
½ tsp ginger, minced

½ tsp orange peel, grated
2 tbsps orange juice
1 tsp pickled green peppercorns,
coarsely ground
½ tsp coriander seeds, roasted
coarsely ground
Salt
Butter

Method

1.   Place 3 tablespoons of butter in a large skillet. Wash the fish fillets, salt them and cook them along with ginger-garlic gently in the butter till tender and white. Remove them carefully onto a glass dish and chill them in the refrigerator.

2.   Chop the cooked prawns finely or pass them through a mincer. Place the minced prawns in a glass bowl. Add the rest of the ingredients, barring the lettuce and the orange slices, and mix well. Chill.

3.   Serve the fish in 8 individual plates. Decorate each plate with lettuce leaves and a slice of orange on one side. Place one fillet next to it and smother it with the prawn sauce.

4.   Serve as a first course with triangles of buttered toast or garlic flavoured French bread.

Curled Fish Fillets in an Almond Sauce

Preparation time: 30 mins   Cooking time: 45-50 mins   Serves: 6-8

Ingredients

4 tbsps self-raising flour
3 whole pomfrets or 12 fish fillets
500 gms Cheddar cheese, grated
15 boiled almonds, flaked, and golden
fried in butter
200 gms canned or fresh sliced
mushrooms

2 litres milk
2 tbsps tabasco sauce
200 gms butter
1 bunch parsley
3 sprigs thyme
1 sour lime
Salt

Method

1.   Cut each pomfret into 4 fillets. You will have 12 fillets. Wash and marinate in salt and the juice of 1 sour lime. Take each fillet by the tail end slowly roll it up and insert toothpicks to allow the roll to retain its shape. After all the fillets have been rolled up, place them in a cool place.

2.   Make a nice thick roux with the butter, milk, parsley, thyme and self-raising flour. Cook it well and add 2 cups of grated cheese to it. Keep aside. Try to get a nice lemony colour by cooking the flour well with the butter before adding the milk. Taste for salt. Never add salt beforehand to any dish when you are using cheese, as the cheese itself contains a lot of salt. Always taste the product and add salt at the end, if required.

3.   Take a rectangular pyrex dish and butter bottom and sides generously. Place the fish rolls leaving gaps in between each.

4.   Whip the cheese sauce, add the canned mushrooms and tabasco and top each roll generously with the sauce. Allow the remaining sauce to cover the base of the dish. Spread the almond flakes onto the dish. Bake in a pre-heated oven at 375°F till golden brown.

5.   Serve with small crisp rolls.

Fish Au Gratin

Preparation time: 25 mins   Cooking time: About 1 Hour   Serves: 6

Ingredients

8 fillets from 2 large pomfrets
Juice of 2 sour limes
½ cup parsley, finely chopped
½ cup chives, cut finely
500 gms potatoes, cooked and mashed
2 cups cheese, grated
2 large tomatoes, skinned, deseeded
and made into pulp

1 litre milk
4 tbsps maida or self-raising flour
1 cup butter
2 tbsps black pepper, coarsely ground
½ tsp chilli powder
2 spring onions, cut in thin rings
Salt

Method

1.   Wash the fish fillets, apply salt, pour the lime juice over them and allow to marinate for 12 minutes.

2.   Place the fillets in a flat pan and cover with spring onions, tomatoes and the chopped parsley and chives. Add 2 cups water and cook till fish is soft. Strain and reserve the fish soup. This should take 10 mins or so.

3.   Place the butter and flour in a pan and stir vigorously. Add the pepper, the milk, ½ litre of the reserved fish soup and make a creamy white sauce. Add half the cheese and stir.

4.   Lay the fish in the centre of a baking dish and pour the sauce over it. Pipe the mashed potato all round the dish and sprinkle a little chilli powder.

5.   Sprinkle the remainder of the grated cheese on top of the sauce so a thick red crust forms when the dish is baked at 350°F in the oven. Make sure the oven is hot when you place the dish inside it. This will take 35-45 mins

6.   Serve with toasted triangles of bread and a green salad.

Pomfret and Prawn Patio ❭

Tandoori Pomfret

Preparation time: 20 mins   Cooking time: 25-30 mins   Serves: 8

Ingredients

4 large pomfrets

1 portion Tandoori masala (see recipe on pg. 3)

3 green chillies

1 tbsp mint, finely chopped

Salt

Oil

Method

1.   Wash the pomfrets and scrub off the scales. Cut below the mouth and remove the entrails and wash the stomach cavity clean.

2.   Rub the fish with salt, a little aji-no-moto and lime juice and set aside to marinate for atleast 2 hours. Make 3 diagonal slashes on each side of the pomfrets.

3.   Grind the chillies and mint with the red masala and coat the pomfrets with this paste. Leave to marinate overnight in your refrigerator.

4.   Thaw the pomfrets. Skewer each pomfret and cook over white-hot coals, basting with a fine dribble of oil when necessary. Remove from heat when golden brown in colour.

5.   Serve with finger chips, lime wedges and tomato slices.

❮ Top: *Fried Surmai Slice*
Below: *Large Tandoori Pomfret*

Pomfret Molee

This is a very light, delicious fish dish and can be made easily at short notice.

Preparation time: 15 mins   Cooking time: 25 mins   Serves: 6-8

Ingredients

Milk of 2 coconuts
2 pomfrets, each cut into 4 or 5 slices
2 onions, finely chopped
1 star anise
Salt
3 tbsps peanut oil

For ground masala paste
(Grind fine in a little water)
10 green chillies, deseeded
10-14 large cloves of garlic
1½ tbsps cumin
½ cup fresh coriander leaves
3 green cardamoms, lightly bruised
5 black peppercorns
1½" amba halad or zedoary
or ginger, finely sliced
3 sprigs curry leaves
3 tbsps lime juice (optional)

Method

1.   Clean the pomfrets by scraping the scales with a knife's edge. Cut into slices and wash them twice. Apply salt and place in a cool spot.

2.   Put the finely chopped onions and curry sprigs into a large mouthed vessel. Add the peanut oil and place on medium heat and cook the onions till pink and soft.

3.   Add the ground masala and stir for 3 minutes until well mixed with the onions. Add the star anise, green cardamoms and the amba halad strips, if available, and stir for 2 more minutes. Lower the flame and add ½ the coconut milk and allow to simmer for 5 minutes. Add the salted fish, raise the heat until the coconut milk boils and add the remaining milk. Taste for salt. Once the fish is boiling, remove from the fire.

4.   Add lime juice, swirl the vessel and serve at once with boiled basmati rice, papads and mango pickle.

Sliced Pomfret in Sweet & Sour Sauce

Preparation time: 15-20 mins   Cooking time: 30-35 mins   Serves: 6-8

Ingredients

2 pomfrets, sliced into 8 to 10 pieces
2 onions, sliced finely and deep fried
2 onions, finely chopped
4 large tomatoes, skinned and finely chopped
½ bunch fresh coriander
1 tbsp Kashmiri chilli powder
2 eggs
½ cup sugarcane vinegar
½ cup sugar

1 cup gram flour
Salt
Oil

For the ground masala paste
(Grind find in a little water)
2 pods garlic
2 tbsps cumin seeds
18 green chillies, deseeded

Method

1.   Cook the two chopped onions in a wide vessel, with 1 cup oil. When the onion becomes soft, add the ground masala and fry it. Then add 1 cup gram flour and chilli powder and stir well. If necessary, add a little extra oil. When the flour becomes a smooth paste, add 3 to 4 cups water and the chopped tomatoes, and stir non-stop till you have a smooth thick gravy.

2.   Wash the fish slices well. Salt them. When the gravy boils and begins to thicken, drop in the fish slices and allow to cook till soft on a low flame. Remove from the flame.

3.   Stir the sugar and vinegar together and add 2 beaten eggs to it. Mix well till the sugar has dissolved and add to the fish gravy in a slow trickle, stirring the sauce carefully to ensure that the fish is not broken, nor the gravy turned into scrambled eggs because of the heat of the sauce. Cover with fried onions and freshly chopped coriander just before serving.

4.   Some people prefer the white type of sauce whilst some prefer this slightly red one. Both taste good. You can substitute salmon slices or prawns for the pomfret slices.

Pomfret Heads in Masala

Preparation time: 12 mins   Cooking time: 15-20 mins   Serves: 4

Ingredients

8 Pomfret heads, each sliced into
two from the centre
2 small onions, finely chopped
4 green chillies, deseeded and finely
chopped
½ fresh coconut, grated and
coarsely ground
1" piece ginger, coarsely ground
1½ tsps sambhar masala
2 tbsps tamarind pulp
Salt
Sesame oil

For the ground masala paste
(Grind fine)
4 Kashmiri chillies
6 large cloves garlic
½" piece turmeric
½ tsp cumin seeds
6 black peppercorns
Rice flour

Method

1.   Wash and salt the pomfret head pieces. Be sure to remove the gills.

2.   Place 2 tablespoons of oil in a vessel over a medium heat. Add the onions and green chillies and cook until the onions are soft and pink. Then add the coarsely ground coconut and ginger and the sambhar powder and stir briskly for 3 to 4 minutes.

3.   Meanwhile, mix the ground masala and tamarind along with 2 teaspoons of rice flour. Apply this to the fish heads.

4.   Add the fish to the onion mixture and gently mix the two. Cover. Place on a low flame. Gently overturn the heads after 5 minutes. Sprinkle 2 to 3 tablespoons of water, cover again for 3 minutes and remove from the fire.

5.   Serve with rice and dal.

Karwari Pomfret Curry

Preparation time: 18 mins   Cooking time: 30 mins   Serves: 4-6

Ingredients

1 large pomfret
2 medium sized onions, sliced fine
1 coconut, grated and divided
into 2 portions
13 Kashmiri chillies, broiled and
deseeded
1 tbsp broiled coriander seeds

1½" piece turmeric
10 black peppercorns
1 tbsp tamarind or
1 large raw mango, peeled and
cut into strips
Rock salt, crushed

Method

1.   Clean the pomfret, remove gills, fins and sides and cut into small 2" pieces. Wash twice and salt the pieces and set aside.

2.   Broil the chillies, coriander seeds, turmeric and black peppercorns. Do not burn any item. Grind very fine along with half the grated coconut and the tamarind.

3.   Remove milk from ½ the leftover grated coconut.

4.   Take a large flat-bottomed vessel. Put in the masala, coconut milk, 1½ cups of water, the mango pieces and salt. Mix well. Crush the sliced onions into the curry mixture and place on a medium flame.

5.   Allow the curry to boil and slide in the fish pieces. Taste for salt. Cook for 7 minutes on high and 3 minutes on low and remove the vessel from the fire.

6.   Serve with boiled rice, onion kachumber and Madrasi rice papads.

Fried Stuffed Pomfret – Kerala Style

Preparation time: 20 mins   Cooking time: 20 mins   Serves: 4-6

Ingredients

1 very large thali or Chinese pomfret, scrape the scales and dirt, leave the fins, tail and head intact. Remove intestines and gills. Wash, make 6 gashes on each side, and apply salt.
Juice of 3 sour limes
¼ tsp mustard seeds
3 tbsps fresh coconut, grated
4 onions, halved and sliced
6 green chillies, deseeded and finely chopped
1 tsp ginger, sliced into fine strips
Salt
Peanut oil

For ground masala paste

(Grind very fine for the pomfret's marinade. Use a little water.)
10 Kashmiri chillies
6 garlic cloves
1" fresh ginger
½ tsp mustard seeds
½ tsp fenugreek seeds
½ tsp cumin seeds
2 onions, finely chopped

Method

1.   Apply the finely ground masala all over the salted pomfret, sprinkle sour lime juice and keep aside in a tray in a cool place for 2 hours.

2.   Place 3 tbsps of oil in a large frying pan over a medium flame. Add ¼ tsp mustard seeds and allow them to pop. Then fry the sliced ginger, onions, chillies, and grated coconut for 8 minutes till golden brown. Add some fine salt, crush the fried items by hand and stuff them into the pomfret. Close the cut with needle and thread or toothpicks.

3.   Pour ¾ cup oil in a large, iron griddle and place over high heat. When the oil bubbles gently, put in the pomfret. Pour the hot oil with a tablespoon on top of the pomfret. Turn over the pomfret when it is golden brown and fry the second side. Remove from the griddle onto a flat dish and serve immediately with chapatis or rice and dal.

Fried Pomfret – Tamil Style

Preparation time: 10 mins   Cooking time: 20 mins   Serves: 4

Ingredients

3 large pomfrets, each cut into
4 to 5 slices
Juice of 3 sour limes
Salt
Peanut oil

For the ground masala paste
(Grind fine in a little water, if necessary)

1 dried coconut piece
8 Kashmiri chillies
4 green chillies
10 black peppercorns
1½ tbsps coriander seeds
1 medium sized onion, chopped fine
2" piece fresh turmeric
10 large cloves garlic
5 curry leaves

Method

1.   Wash the pomfret slices twice. Marinade in salt and lime juice for ½ hour.

2.   Dry roast the masala on an iron tava over low heat for 7 minutes and then, grind very fine.

3.   Apply the masala to the pomfret slices and fry a few of them at a time in hot oil on a tava or non-stick skillet till golden brown.

4.   Serve as an accompaniment to rice and dal.

Pomfret Tails with Spinach

Preparation time: 10 mins   Cooking time: 15-20 mins   Serves: 4

Ingredients

6 pomfret tails
1 small onion, sliced into rings
10 leaves spinach
1 tsp broiled coriander seeds
Salt
Butter

For the ground masala paste
(Grind into a paste)
5 green chillies, deseeded
6 large cloves garlic
1 tsp cumin seeds
Seeds of 1 green cardamom

Method

1. Wash the pomfret tails and salt them.

2. Drop the spinach leaves for 2 minutes in boiling water and drain them in a sieve.

3. Place 2 tablespoons of butter in a flat vessel and add the onion rings. Place on medium heat. Stir till the onion softens, then add the ground masala and stir for 5 minutes on a low flame.

4. Add the pomfret tails and turn them over once. Then spread the spinach leaves on top of the tails and cover and cook for 7 minutes. Stir and overturn the tails and leaves. Taste for salt. Sprinkle the broiled coriander seeds on top of the tails.

5. Serve hot with buttered toast.

Pomfret Pickle

Preparation time: 25 mins   Cooking time: 30-35 mins   Serves: 10

Ingredients

2 large pomfrets (Discard head, fins, gills, stomach pieces).
2 tbsps broiled cumin
1 tsp mustard seeds
1 cup jaggery, crushed
6 green chillies, ground
12 black peppercorns, ground
Salt
Sesame oil

For the ground masala paste
(Grind in strong vinegar)
1" piece turmeric
16 Kashmiri chillies, deseeded
2" piece ginger
10 large cloves garlic

Method

1.   Cut the pomfrets into slices and each slice into 2 pieces. Wash and salt the pieces of fish and apply the ground green chillies and peppercorns.

2.   Place 1 cup oil in a large vessel on medium heat. When hot, add the ground masala and stir for 3 minutes. Then lower the flame and allow to simmer for 5 minutes. Add 1 cup vinegar and bring the mixture to a boil. Add the crushed jaggery and allow it to melt.

3.   Then gently mix in the pomfret pieces and shake the vessel round and round so that all the pieces are well coated with the masala.

4.   Allow to simmer gently for 10 minutes.

5.   Cool and store in a glass jar.

Fish, Prawn, Eggs & Mushroom Pulao

Although from the list of things you need for this pulao, the recipe appears daunting – don't worry, it is simple and straight-forward. To the inexperienced cook, it will take a little time to get all the items together.

Preparation time: 35 mins   Cooking time: 1 Hour   Serves: 8-10

Ingredients

700 gms basmati rice
2 gms saffron
3 onions, sliced and fried
3 bay leaves
4 green cardamoms, crushed
2" stick cinnamon
3 star anise
Salt
1 tbsp ghee

For the Prawns:

30 fresh medium sized prawns, shelled, deveined and washed thrice
18 curry leaves
Salt
Oil

For the Mushrooms:

200 gms mushrooms soaked in water for ½ hour, sliced and salted

For the Fish Fillets:

20 small pomfret fillets or any other fish
3 sour limes
1 tbsp black pepper powder
1 tbsp coriander leaves, freshly cut
4-5 eggs
Breadcrumbs
Salt
Oil

For the ground masala paste

(Grind fine with ½ cup water)
8 red chillies
½ large pod garlic
½" piece ginger
1 tsp cumin seeds
1 tsp coriander seeds
½ tsp mustard seeds

1 tbsp salted butter

For the Boiled Eggs:

9 eggs, boiled, each cut into two
Breadcrumbs
1 cup gram flour
½ tsp baking powder
Salt
Oil

For the chutney paste

(Grind with ¼ cup thick tamarind water)
¼ fresh coconut, grated
1 bunch fresh coriander
¼ bunch fresh mint
½ tsp cumin seeds
1" fresh ginger

For the Layering of the Pulao:

2 large onions, finely chopped
2 large onions, sliced
1200 gms large tomatoes, skinned, deseeded and pulped
1½ tsps red reshampatti chilli powder
2 tsps garam masala
1½ tbsps sugar

1 tsp crushed coriander seeds
150 gms raisins, washed
200 gms carrots, cut into small pieces
200 gms potatoes
½ bunch coriander, finely chopped
Salt
Pure ghee

Method

1. Cook the rice with saffron, onions, bay leaves, cardamoms, star anise, salt and ghee. When cooked, spread on a flat plate and cool.

2. Fry the sliced onions for layering the pulao and keep aside.

3. Boil the carrots and potatoes in hot, salted water until tender. Drain through a colander and set aside.

4. Place the chopped onions in a vessel along with 3 tablespoons of ghee.

5. When the onions become soft, add the chilli powder, garam masala and coriander seeds. Lower the flame and add the tomato pulp and bring to a boil. Add the sugar, washed raisins, chopped coriander and the boiled potatoes and carrots. Taste for salt. Allow to simmer for 10 minutes and remove from the fire.

6.   Wash the fish fillets twice and marinate in salt, lemon juice and black pepper. Sprinkle freshly cut coriander over the fillets so the leaves stick to the fish. Place a frying pan half full of oil on a medium flame. Spread the breadcrumbs on a wooden board and coat the fillets on both sides. Whisk the eggs and when the oil heats up, dip each fillet in the eggs and add to the oil. Fry till golden brown and set aside. You will need to fry them in 3 or 4 batches.

7.   Wash the prawns thrice. Add salt. Apply the ground masala and keep aside for an hour. Cook the prawns in 2 tablespoons oil and curry leaves and the water with which you wash your grinding stone or mixie. Cook till thick. Taste for salt.

8.   Cut each of the boiled eggs into two vertical pieces. Coat with the thick chutney paste. Make a batter with 1½ cups of water, salt, baking powder and gram flour, it should not be very thin. Roll each chutney-egg piece into the breadcrumbs, then dip into the gram flour batter and fry in hot oil. Place in the same pan in which you had fried the fillets. Allow the eggs to become golden red and then remove from the fire and set aside to cool.

9.   Heat butter lightly and add the washed, sliced, salted mushrooms. Stir fry for 5 minutes and remove from the fire.

10. Take a large biryani vessel. Add some ghee to the bottom of the vessel and spread it over the sides. Divide the rice into 4 portions. Place one portion at the bottom of the vessel and arrange the fillets on top of the rice.

11. Divide the tomato gravy into 3 parts. Sprinkle one portion over the fillets and cover with another layer of rice. Sprinkle all the prawns and the prawn gravy over the rice. Cover with the third layer of rice, and layer the fried eggs over it. Cover with one portion of the tomato gravy. Cover this with the fourth portion of rice and place all the mushrooms over it. Cover the mushrooms with the third portion of the tomato gravy and sprinkle the fried onions. Cover with foil or a tight fitting lid and dough, place on an iron tava over a medium flame for 30 minutes before serving.

    This pulao needs no accompaniments except some raw onion kachumber and kulfi with long strands of coloured falooda for dessert.

Fish, Prawn, Eggs and Mushroom Pulao ›

Pomfret and Prawn Patio

Preparation time: 15-20 mins   Cooking time: 35-45 mins   Serves: 6-8

Ingredients

300 gms large deveined prawns
10 slices pomfret fish
2 large onions, chopped
4 large tomatoes, chopped
10 cherry tomatoes
10 baby brinjals
4 drumsticks cut into 4 pieces each
2 capsicums, sliced
½ cup vinegar
½ cup jaggery
½ cup fresh coriander, chopped
1 sprig curry leaves
4 slit green chillies
Salt
1 cup sesame oil
1 cup refined oil

For the ground masala paste

(Grind together in ½ cup vinegar)
12 large Kashmiri chillies
½ coconut, fresh grated
2 tbsps cumin seeds
1 large pod garlic
8 black peppercorns
1 tbsp Parsi dhansakh masala
1 tsp mustard seeds
1 tbsp raw mango pickle
Sambhar powder

Method

1. Wash the pomfret and prawns separately, apply salt and set aside.

2. Put the sesame oil, onions, and curry leaves in a heavy flat-bottomed vessel and allow the leaves to crackle. Cook till onions are soft. Add chopped tomatoes, the ground masala, slit green chillies to the pan and cook over gentle heat. Add the prawns and cook them over a slow fire. Add 2 cups of water. When the prawns

◀ *Top left: Vegetable Khichdi*
Top right: Fish Cakes
Below: Pomfret Slices in Sweet and Sour Sauce

are cooked, add the fish and crushed jaggery. Sway the vessel from side to side by holding the vessel with 2 napkins. Do not stir with a spoon. Add more salt only if necessary as the pomfret and prawns are already salted. Add cherry tomatoes. Remove from the fire.

3.   Cut the brinjals into 4 pieces. Retain from the stalk. Place in salted water. Cut the capsicums into slices. Heat 1 cup refined oil in a frying pan. Fry the baby brinjals and allow the oil to drain on a plate. Put the capsicum slices in the same pan and remove immediately from the oil. Boil the drumsticks in salted water and set aside. Chop the coriander.

4.   Serve the patia fish by placing the prawns, fish slices and gravy on a flat dish. Decorate it with the fried baby brinjals, capsicums, drumsticks and coriander. Serve with hot parathas or boiled rice and plain yellow dal.

Halwa in Sweet & Sour Sauce

Preparation time: 7 mins   Cooking time: 35 mins   Serves: 4-6

Ingredients

1 very large halwa, cleaned and cut
into pieces and washed twice.
Do not eat the skin.
3 large onions, 2 chopped fine, 1 sliced
and deep fried till golden
3 tomatoes, skinned and cut fine
½ cup fresh chopped coriander leaves
3 tbsps rice flour or gram flour
½ cup vinegar
2 tbsps sugar

3-4 eggs
Salt
Sesame oil

For the ground masala paste
(Grind fine in sugarcane vinegar)
10 large cloves garlic
10 green chillies, deseeded
2 tbsps cumin seeds

Method

1.   Salt the washed fish. Keep aside.

2.   Heat 3 tablespoons of oil in a large vessel. When the oil gets hot, add the onions and keep stirring non-stop until they become soft and pink. Should not brown.

3.   Add the ground masala and tomatoes and stir well and cook for 5 minutes over low heat. Add 2 to 3 large glasses of water according to the amount of gravy you desire. Add salt and allow to boil.

4.   When the gravy boils, add the salted fish pieces and cook them for 5 minutes.

5.   Beat 2 eggs till frothy, add half a cup of vinegar and 2 tablespoons of sugar. Mix well till the sugar has dissolved. Then lower the flame, stir carefully and taste for salt.

6.   Mix the flour into the vinegar mixture and slowly pour into the hot masala gravy, stirring non-stop. There should be no flour lumps. The gravy should be as smooth as silk. Hold the vessel with 2 kitchen napkins and keep swirling the sauce and fish around for 5 minutes till the sauce boils and the fish is cooked.

7.   Serve with hot chapatis or ghee khichdi.

Fried Halwa or Black Pomfret

This is a rich, fatty fish, very delicious to the taste. But also very dangerous if the skin is eaten. The results could be disastrous.

When you buy the fish in the market, check the eyes and gills. Both should be shining. The gills should be bright red and glistening. Never buy frozen halwas. As soon as you bring it home, scale it, cut off its head and sides and slice it. Then wash it thoroughly with rice flour. Apply salt and masalas and cook it as soon as you can.

Do not buy stale halwa. The simplest and tastiest way to cook this fish is to fry it on an iron tava or griddle.

Preparation time: 10 mins   Cooking time: 10-15 mins   Serves: 4

Ingredients

1 large halwa, cut into 6-8 slices   ½ tbsp black pepper powder
2 tbsps red chilli powder   Salt
1 tbsp turmeric powder   Sesame oil

Method

1.   Clean the fish, cut off the head, scrub the scales off, remove the gills and intestines and slice the halwa or cut into small pieces. Wash well twice.

2.   Apply salt, turmeric, chilli and pepper powders.

3.   Heat oil in a tava or iron frying pan and fry the halwa in small batches.

4.   Serve with sour lime wedges, chanadal and hot chapattis; or serve the halwa with vegetable khichdi and curd curry.

Halwa in Plain Gravy

Preparation time: 20 mins   Cooking time: 20 mins   Serves: 4-6

Ingredients

1 very large halwa, cleaned and cut into 2" pieces (The head can be used)

½ coconut milk

5 pieces kokam

3 sprigs curry leaves

Coarse salt

Peanut oil

For the ground masala paste

(Grind fine in water)

½ coconut, grated

2 large onions, grated

6-8 green chillies, deseeded and chopped fine

1 tbsp cumin seeds

1 tbsp coriander seeds

1 tbsp aniseeds

1½" fresh ginger

Method

1.   Wash the fish pieces well. Salt them and set aside.

2.   Place the curry sprigs and ½ cup of oil into a large flat-bottomed vessel. Place on medium flame. When the leaves start crackling, put in the ground masala and fry it over low heat for 7 minutes. Put in the fish pieces, stir for 2 minutes and add 2 glasses of water and allow to cook for 5 to 7 minutes, until the gravy starts bubbling. Taste for salt.

3.   Add the washed kokam pieces to the gravy and then pour in the coconut milk. Cook until the gravy boils well – which should take atleast 7 more minutes.

4.   Serve hot with boiled rice and papads.

5.   Remember not to eat the skin.

The Prawns

Prawns belong to the class Crustacea and come under the order Decapoda.

These crustaceans are very important economically as they comprise amongst the best food items under marine food resources. They are in great demand in the home market and support a very valuable export market.

Prawns are broadly divided into Penaeid and non-Penaeid varieties. The Penaeid are very important, because they grow to a large size, which is good for export trade. The non-Penaeid come under several families. "Prawns" are Penaeidae and the others have to be called "shrimps" as they belong to smaller species of other families.

The prawns are of particular importance in Maharashtra and Gujarat because they are caught here in great numbers.

Mostly they are marketed fresh.

In the process of freezing, prawns are beheaded and deveined before being graded and packed in cartons. The larger ones are frozen in their shells.

Prawn Cocktails

Prawn Cocktails are best served chilled in champagne goblets. They are a gourmet's delight. 3 types of cocktails are given here.

Preparation time: 20 mins   Cooking time: nil   Serves: 6-8

1. *Zingy Prawn Cocktail*

Ingredients

6 champagne glasses chilled in the refrigerator
Iceberg or cos lettuce leaves
2 cups mayonnaise
2 tbsps tabasco sauce

4 tbsps tomato ketchup
2 tbsps gherkins, finely chopped
500 gms cleaned, washed, deveined prawns, cooked in a mixture of water, tomato sauce, salt and chilled well

Method

1. Cut the lettuce into shreds or small pieces after washing the leaves and allowing them to dry. Place in the refrigerator.

2. Drain the prawns from the tomato and water liquid.

3. Place the mayonnaise, tabasco sauce, tomato ketchup and finely chopped gherkins in a large glass bowl. Mix gently. Add the prawns. Mix again. Taste for salt. Refrigerate.

4. Five minutes before you serve the cocktails, divide the lettuce amongst the champagne goblets. Fill each goblet to the brim with the chilled prawns in the cocktail sauce and serve immediately.

5. If you like, you may top each glass with whipped cream and a cherry.

2. Prawn Cocktail With Avocadoes

1.   Everything is the same as above, except that one finely chopped avocado is added to the cocktail sauce and the gherkins are omitted.

2.   Gently mix in 200 gms cream before chilling the sauce. Taste for salt.

3. Prawn Cocktail With Finely Chopped Black Olives

1.   Everything is the same except that the gherkins and avocado are substituted with half a cup of finely chopped black olives.

2.   Instead of the cream, mix in 1 cup of chopped fresh, sour and salty paneer.

Prawn Salad

Serve at lunch time at a patio party or garden party for friends.

Preparation time: 25 mins   Cooking time: 7 mins   Serves: 6-8

Ingredients

500 gms large shelled prawns,
boiled in salted water and
½ cup tomato ketchup

2 large apples, peeled and diced

4 hard boiled eggs, chopped

4 large red tomatoes, skinned and sliced

450 gms button mushrooms,
sliced and cooked in butter

4 tbsps balsamic vinegar

2 tbsps gelatine

1 cup hot boiling water

2 tbsps chopped parsley

4 large tomatoes, skinned and
crushed fine

Salt

8 red radishes (optional)

Method

1.   Dissolve the gelatine in the hot water and mix well in a bowl till melted. Add the crushed tomatoes. Taste for salt.

2.   To the above mixture, add the mushrooms, apples, prawns, eggs and the parsley and mix well.

3.   Take a mould and oil it well. Put the prawn mixture into it and smoothen the top. Cover with the sliced tomatoes and chill for 4 hours.

4.   To unmould, dip the mould for 2 minutes in boiling water and empty the contents over a salver covered with lettuce leaves and decorate with red radishes.

Bengal Toast

Preparation time: 30 mins   Cooking time: 30 mins   Serves: 10-15

Ingredients

400 gms shelled, deveined, washed prawns

1 small sliced bread

4 large onions, minced

1 cup fresh coriander, minced

¼ cup fresh mint, minced

6 green chillies, deseeded and minced

1½ tsps chilli powder

1 tsp turmeric powder (fresh pounded turmeric, if available)

1 tsp dhansakh masala

¾ cup sugarcane vinegar

½ cup brown sugar

Salt

Ghee or oil

Method

1.   Deep fry the bread slices and set aside.

2.   Place the minced onion in a frying pan with ½ cup of oil and cook till pink over a low flame. If necessary, add 1 tablespoon of oil so the onions don't burn.

3.   Add the prawns and salt. Cover and cook for 10 minutes. When soft, add the fresh coriander, mint and green chillies, as well as the chilli powder, turmeric and dhansakh masala. Stir well and keep covered over a slow fire for 10 minutes. Keep stirring so that the prawns don't stick to the pan.

4.   Add the sugar and vinegar and taste for salt. Keep stirring the mixture till it thickens. Spread on the fried toasts and serve hot.

Prawn Bhajias or Batter Fried Prawns

Preparation time: 10 mins   Cooking time: 20-25 mins   Serves: 6-8

Ingredients

2 cups fresh prawns, deveined

1½ cups gram flour

1 large onion, finely chopped

6 green chillies, finely chopped

½ cup fresh coriander, finely chopped

2 tbsps mint, finely chopped

2 tsps red chilli powder

1 tsp turmeric powder

1 tsp dhansakh masala

1 pinch cooking soda

2 sour limes, juice only

1 tbsp sugar

Salt

Oil

Method

1. Mash the prawns with a sharp knife, apply salt and place in a flat dish. Add all the ingredients and salt to taste and mix well with ½ cup of water. Make a nice soft dough and roll into little balls with wet hands. If mixture is too tight, add a little water.

2. Place oil in a deep frying pan and when hot drop in 10 to 15 balls at a time. Fry till red and drain in a colander.

3. Serve with green coconut or tamarind chutney.

Prawn Kababs

Preparation time: 10 mins   Cooking time: 20 mins   Serves: 4-6

Ingredients

2 cups prawns, shelled, deveined, coarsely ground
1 medium sized onion, chopped
2 eggs, beaten
Juice of 1 lemon
¼ bunch coriander, washed and chopped
½ cup breadcrumbs/flour
Salt
Oil

For the ground masala paste
(Grind fine)
2 large boiled potatoes
1 tbsp cumin seeds
10 black peppercorns
6 green chillies, deseeded
1 tsp poppy seeds
8-10 cloves garlic

Method

1.   Grind finely cumin, garlic, green chillies, peppercorns, poppy seeds and boiled potatoes into a firm paste without using any water. Add coarsely ground prawns to it. Salt to taste. Mix well.

2.   Chop the onion very fine. Mix together the stiffly beaten eggs, juice of one lemon, onion and chopped coriander. Fold this into the ground prawn mixture. Mix thoroughly and divide into little round balls. Wet your hands whilst making the balls to get a smooth finish. Coat with breadcrumbs or any other flour and deep-fry in hot oil. Take care not to fry too many at one time.

3.   Serve as appetizers with drinks, or with masala dal and rice or any vegetable dish at meal times.

Chilli Hot Prawns

Preparation time: 20 mins   Cooking time: 15-20 mins   Serves: 4-6

Ingredients

600 gms prawns
1 tbsp garlic, finely minced
1 tbsp ginger, finely minced
1 pinch aji-no-moto
2 tbsps tomato sauce
2 tbsps soya bean sauce
2½ cups water
1 lettuce head
½ cup sugarcane vinegar
Salt
Sesame oil

For the ground masala paste
(Grind together)
16 large cloves garlic
10 red chillies, preferably Kashmir
2 tbsps sesame seeds

Method

1.   Wash the prawns twice. Retain head and tail shell. Remove shell from the center portion and devein. Wash again and marinate in salt and soya bean sauce for 2 hours.

2.   Place 2½ cups of water in a flat vessel. Add the prawns, ginger, garlic, aji-no-moto and tomato sauce and bring to a boil. Once prawns are tender, remove from the fire.

3.   Grind the garlic, chillies, sesame seeds in the vinegar and cook it for 10 minutes over a low fire in ½ cup of sesame oil.

4.   Place finely chopped lettuce in a bowl and arrange the prawns with their heads up. Sprinkle the hot sauce on top of the prawns and serve.

Shrimps Cooked with Brinjals

Preparation time: 12 mins   Cooking time: 25-30 mins   Serves: 4

Ingredients

2 medium sized brinjals, peeled
2 bunches spring onions
2 green chillies
1 cup shrimps, shelled
¼ cup fresh coriander, chopped
½ cup spinach

½ tsp turmeric powder
1 heaped tbsp ginger-garlic paste
¼ tsp oregano
Salt
Oil

Method

1.   Cut the brinjals into tiny pieces and soak in salted water. Finely chop the spring onions and spinach.

2.   Place the onions in a deep frying pan with ½ cup oil. When cooked and transparent, add oregano, the ginger-garlic paste, salt and the brinjal pieces. Throw away the salt water. Cover and cook over a low fire. When the brinjals are half-cooked, add the shrimps, turmeric powder, spinach and green chillies. Cover and allow the brinjals to become soft and tender. When the brinjal is soft and mushy, mix well and add the fresh coriander.

3.   Serve with lemon wedges and hot parathas.

4.   If available, use one chopped green mango, whilst cooking the brinjal and shrimps.

Goanese Prawn Cutlets

Preparation time: 25 mins   Cooking time: 20-24 mins   Serves: 6-8

Ingredients

450 gms shelled, deveined, washed prawns
3 onions, chopped fine
3 eggs
Breadcrumbs
Salt
Peanut Oil

For the ground masala paste
(Grind fine with the lime juice)
½ large coconut, grated
1" piece ginger
4 green chillies, deseeded
3 red chillies, deseeded
1 tsp cumin seeds
1 tsp coriander seeds
¼ cup fresh coriander leaves
3 cardamoms, seeds only
1½" cinnamon
2 cloves
7 black peppercorns
Juice of 2 sour limes

Method

1.   Place the prawns in a small vessel, salt them and lightly dry them over very low heat for 5 minutes. Grind the prawns coarsely. Place in a flat dish and mix with the ground masala. Add the onions and mix and taste for salt.

2.   Make large even-sized balls out of the prawn mixture. Place breadcrumbs on a wooden board. Roll the balls, one at a time, in the breadcrumbs and make oval shaped cutlets by pressing with a flat knife.

3.   Place a deep frying pan, half filled with oil on a medium flame and allow to get hot.

4.   Whisk the eggs one at a time. Dip the cutlets into the egg and immerse in the hot oil and fry till golden brown, in small batches.

5.   Serve with any vegetable or black masoor dal.

Tandoori Tiger Prawns

Preparation time: 25 mins   Cooking time: 25-30 mins   Serves: 6-9

Ingredients

20 large tiger prawns
Juice of 2 sour limes
½ tsp asafoetida, powdered
½ tsp fried mustard seeds
200 gms thick yoghurt
1 banana leaf cut in the shape
of a lotus leaf
10 tomato skin roses
Salt
Oil

For the ground masala paste

(Grind to a paste in ¼ cup vinegar)
4 Kashmiri chillies
1 tsp black peppercorns
1 tsp broiled coriander seeds
1 tsp broiled cumin seeds

Method

1.   Shell and devein the prawns and wash them thrice. Apply salt and the lime juice. Let this marinate for 2 hours.

2.   Grind the masala into a soft paste. Add the asafoetida, fried mustard seeds and the yoghurt. Mix well and apply to the prawns, coating well. Marinate overnight in the freezer.

3.   Thaw the prawns. Make roses out of the tomato skins of 10 hard tomatoes. Arrange these roses on the banana leaf, place on a glass dish.

4.   Grill the prawns till cooked soft. Arrange the prawns between the roses on the banana leaf and serve with whiskey or rum as an appetizer.

Tandoori Tiger Prawns ❯

Prawn Stuffed Omelettes

Preparation time: 8 mins   Cooking time: 30 mins   Serves: 4-6

Ingredients

For the Omelettes:

8 eggs
¼ tsp pepper
½ tsp chilli powder
Salt
Ghee

For the Stuffing:

1 stalk celery, finely chopped
1 cup prawns, deveined and washed
2 large tomatoes, skinned and deseeded
2 green chillies, deseeded and
finely chopped
4 spring onions or a packet of chives

Method

1.   Chop the spring onions, celery and skinned tomatoes finely and cook in 2 tablespoons of ghee till soft.

2.   Add the prawns, chilli powder, deseeded green chillies and salt to taste and cook till the mixture is thick and prawns soft.

3.   Beat the eggs, two at a time, with a pinch of pepper powder and salt in your mixie and pour into a non-stick pan in which you have heated 1 tablespoon ghee. Shake the pan and allow the omelette to cook over a slow fire till settled.

4.   Divide the prawn mixture into four portions. Place ¼ of it on ½ of the omelette as it is cooking. When the bottom side is fairly firm, place a spatula below the omelette which has no filling and invert it over the stuffed half. Cook for a couple of minutes more, overturn and then slide it onto a plate and serve immediately. Make the three other omelettes in the same manner.

❮ *Top: Prawn Fried Rice*
Below: Prawn Stuffed Omelette

Prawn Patio

This is a great delicacy for sea-food lovers and will keep for a week if cooked only in vinegar and without the addition of onions and tomatoes.

Preparation time: 15 mins   Cooking time: 25-35 mins   Serves: 4-6

Ingredients

2 cups shelled deveined prawns
3 large onions, finely chopped
10 cherry tomatoes
2 capsicums, cut into small squares
½ tsp turmeric powder
1 tbsp dhansakh masala
Curry leaves
50 gms jaggery

For the ground masala paste
(Grind in ½ cup vinegar)
10-12 Kashmiri chillies, deseeded
1 large pod garlic
1 tbsp cumin seeds
½ tsp mustard seeds
1 tsp peppercorns

Method

1.   Grind the masala to a soft consistency using as much vinegar as necessary.

2.   Fry the chopped onion in ½ cup of oil till golden. Add the ground masala, turmeric, dhansakh masala, curry leaves and cook it over a low flame. Add the prawns and fry in the masala. When it becomes dry, add the jaggery, any remaining vinegar, the cherry tomatoes, capsicums and one cup water. Simmer till cooked.

3.   Sprinkle fresh coriander and serve with parathas or the famous Parsi Dhan-Dar or white rice and yellow dal.

Ladyfingers Cooked with Prawns

Preparation time: 15 mins   Cooking time: 30-35 mins   Serves: 4-6

Ingredients

300 gms ladyfingers
1 cup prawns, deveined
2 onions, finely chopped
2 tomatoes, finely chopped
1 cup coriander leaves
2 tbsps mint, chopped
1 tsp chilli powder

1 tsp amchur powder
1 tsp turmeric powder
½ tsp cumin seeds, ground
1 tsp sesame seeds
½ tsp mustard seeds
Salt
Oil

Method

1.   Wash the prawns, apply salt and set aside. Wash and dry the ladyfingers and cut into slices, a quarter of an inch thick.

2.   Place ½ cup of oil in a frying pan and cook the onions in it till pink and soft. Add the chilli and turmeric powders, cumin, sesame and mustard seeds. Stir well and add the prawns. Cover and cook for a few minutes. Add ½ cup of water, coriander, tomatoes and mint. Cover and cook till the prawns soften.

3.   Put oil in a separate frying pan. Apply salt to the ladyfingers and deep fry. Drain. Cover the cooked prawns with the ladyfingers, amchur powder and allow to simmer for 5 minutes. Mix before serving.

Prawns and Cottage Cheese Casserole

Preparation time: 20 mins   Cooking time: 40 mins   Serves: 6

Ingredients

2 cups large prawns, deveined
and salted
300 gms cottage cheese
½ bunch fresh coriander
2 large onions, chopped fine
2 tbsps green chillies, chopped fine
3 tbsps butter
¼ tsp oregano

½ tsp mustard seeds
½ tsp caraway seeds
2 tsps chilli powder
½ cup tomato pulp
2 sprigs curry leaves
7 peppercorns, coarsely ground
Salt
Oil

Method

1.   Heat 3 tablespoons butter in a heavy bottomed pan. Add the chopped onions and cook until soft. Add the curry leaves, oregano, caraway, mustard seeds and allow them to pop. Quickly toss in the powdered spices, green chillies, finely pulped tomatoes and prawns. Turn the heat low and allow to simmer for 15-20 minutes, adding ½ cup of water if necessary, till the prawns are tender. Add the chopped coriander.

2.   Cut the cottage cheese into bite size cubes. Heat a frying pan half full with oil. When the oil is hot, gently slide in the paneer cubes in 2 batches. Remove with a slotted spoon when golden brown and immediately put it in the cooked prawn mixture. Stir well.

3.   Place the prawn and cottage cheese mixture onto a heated dish and serve immediately with hot chapattis or yellow rice.

Red Pumpkin and Prawn Casserole

Preparation time: 15 mins   Cooking time: 25 mins   Serves: 8-10

Ingredients

2 cups prawns, deveined

1 kg. red pumpkin

250 gms ripe tomatoes

4 green chillies, deseeded

2 tbsps coriander, chopped

2 sprigs curry leaves

1½" ginger, finely chopped

1 tsp cumin seeds, coarsely ground

½ tsp turmeric powder

3 tsps chilli powder

¼ tsp mustard seeds

juice of ½ sour lime

2 tsps sugar

Salt

3 tbsps ghee

Method

1.   Peel the pumpkin, cut into large square pieces and boil in 4 cups of water, until soft. Grind to a soft smooth pulp through a sieve or moulé legume.

2.   Chop the green chillies and ginger finely. Peel the tomatoes and cut into small pieces.

3.   Heat the ghee in a flat shallow pan and add the mustard seeds and curry leaves. Allow to splutter then lower heat and add green chillies, ginger, cumin seeds, turmeric and chilli powders. Stir, add the tomatoes and prawns and then cover and allow to cook over a low fire for at least 15-20 minutes after which the pumpkin pulp should be added. Cover and cook for another 10 minutes. Salt to taste.

4.   Just before serving, add the juice of ½ sour lime and 2 teaspoons sugar. Sprinkle with chopped coriander and serve.

Brinjals Baked with Cheese and Prawns

Preparation time: 20 mins   Cooking time: 45-55 mins   Serves: 8

Ingredients

2 tbsps coriander, chopped

2 eggs, beaten well

2 egg yolks

4 large black seedless brinjals

2 sour limes

2 cups prawns, deveined and boiled

½ litre milk

350 gms butter

2 cups cheese, grated

4 chillies, deseeded and chopped

2 large tomatoes, skinned and deseeded

¼ tsp mace powder

¼ tsp nutmeg powder

1 tsp chilli powder

4 tbsps self-raising flour

Salt

Method

1.   Take 100 gms butter and put it on a hot skillet. When it begins to melt, add the tomatoes, boiled prawns, green chillies, nutmeg, mace and chilli powders. Cover and cook over a slow fire till soft. Taste for salt, add the coriander, stir and set aside.

2.   Make a roux out of the remaining butter, flour, cheese and milk, reserving a cup of cheese and 2 tablespoons of the butter.

3.   Wash the brinjals and slit them into halves horizontally, keeping the stalks intact. Scoop out some of the flesh and make a little hollow in each half of the brinjals. Squeeze out the lime juice and mix with a little salt. Apply this to the inside of the brinjals. Steam in a colander with the scooped-out side facing downwards. Cook till the brinjal is almost done but still firm.

4.   Grease a rectangular pyrex dish or aluminium tray lavishly with butter. Beat the eggs well and mix into the prawns along with the roux or white sauce and fill the hollow of the brinjals with this mixture. Place the brinjals in the dish. Do not flatten the mixture but let it bulge out. Smoothen the surface with the beaten egg-yolks and sprinkle with the reserved cheese. Bake in a preheated oven at 350°F till the top is golden brown.

5.   Serve immediately before the bake loses its fluffiness.

Prawn Pappas from Kerala

Preparation time: 20 mins   Cooking time: 22 mins   Serves: 6-8

Ingredients

500 gms shelled, deveined prawns
½ tsp mustard seeds
3 sprigs curry leaves
Juice of 2 sour limes or
5 pieces kokum
Salt
½ cup peanut oil

For the ground masala paste
(Grind very fine with a little water)
½ fresh coconut, grated
8 reshampatti chillies
1" fresh or dry turmeric
1½ tbsp broiled coriander seeds
½ tsp broiled fenugreek seeds
7 black peppercorns
5 small onions, coarsely chopped
2 green chillies, deseeded and chopped
10 large garlic cloves

Method

1. Place the prawns in a colander and wash well. Add coarse salt and set aside.

2. Take a heavy bottomed pan and add the curry sprigs and oil and place over medium heat. When the leaves crackle, add the mustard seeds and mix them in the hot oil for 1 minute. Then add the ground masala and stir for 3 minutes until it turns a red hot colour. Then add the prawns, mix well with the masala and lower the heat. Cover and cook for 3 minutes. Then add 1½ cups of water and allow to simmer till dry. Taste for salt.

3. Serve hot with boiled rice or parathas along with a cucumber and onion salad.

Ladyfingers Stuffed with Shrimps – Goanese Style

Preparation time: 25 mins   Cooking time: 15 mins   Serves: 4-6

Ingredients

450 gms tender but large ladyfingers

400 gms shelled, washed baby shrimps, lightly pounded

6 cloves garlic

1 cup fresh coconut, grated

2 small onions, finely chopped

10 Begdi chillies

1 tbsp coriander seeds

1 tsp turmeric powder

1 tsp sambhar powder

2 tsps poppy seeds

1 tsp garam masala

Juice of 2 sour limes

2 tbsps fresh coriander leaves, finely chopped

Salt

Peanut Oil

Method

1.   Clean the shrimps, wash twice, salt them lightly and set aside. Wash the ladyfingers, dry them in a colander or on a kitchen napkin.

2.   Place 3 teaspoons oil in a non-stick frying pan and roast the chillies, coriander seeds and poppy seeds in it till a delicious aroma arises. Do not allow to singe.

3.   Grind the coconut, garlic, chillies, coriander seeds, poppy seeds and the 3 powdered masalas as fine as you can. Grind one onion to a pulp and mix into the ground paste. Add the pounded shrimps to the ground masala with salt and lime juice and mix well. Mix in the small chopped onion.

4.   Cut each ladyfinger down one side only. Stuff the shrimp masala into the cut wedge without tearing the ladyfinger. Stuff all the vegetable in the same manner and lightly sprinkle with salt.

5.   Heat oil in a large frying pan. When hot, fry the ladyfingers in small portions till golden brown. Remove from the hot oil and serve at once. Eat these ladyfingers for breakfast or lunch.

6.   If any shrimp masala is left over, mix in some mashed potato or soaked, squeezed bread, make round balls, cover with beaten egg and deep fry till golden brown.

Prawn Stuffed Avocadoes

Avocadoes have a unique acquired taste that is not sweet but flavourful and with a smooth, creamy texture. They are very popular in America. However, in India they are only recently gaining popularity. My friend Amy Jehangir, who lives in Khandala, has a tree in her garden and ever since I met her, I have enjoyed eating this fruit in salads.

An avocado is ripe when its flesh is firm, shining and typically greenish yellow. It turns brown very quickly after exposure to air. To prevent this, lemon juice is added to an avacado after it is cut into two horizontal pieces. Once the large seed is removed, the two centres in each half can be stuffed with fillings as desired.

Preparation time: 20 mins   Serves: 8

Ingredients

4 avocados
1 cup prawns, deveined, boiled, cooked
3 hard boiled eggs, chopped
4 gherkins, chopped
1 stalk celery, chopped finely

1 tbsp tabasco sauce
4 sliced tomatoes
1 cup mayonnaise
1 tbsp fresh dill, chopped
Salt

Method

1.   Cut each avocado into two pieces. Remove the seed in the centre. Rub each cut piece with lime juice.

2.   Mix all the items except the tomatoes, together in a bowl and chill the mixture for 2 hours.

3.   Just before serving, place each avocado half on a plate decorated with tomato slices. Fill the centre with the cold mixture and serve as a starter.

4.   You can substitute boiled, flaked chicken for the prawns or bits of cheese and pineapple.

Tiger Prawns and Ripe Mango Salad

Preparation time: 25 mins   Cooking time: 30 mins   Serves: 8-10

Ingredients

6 ripe, skinned alphonso mangoes, flesh sliced

20 large deveined tiger prawns

2 avocados, sliced

1 cup mayonnaise

¼ cup parsley, finely chopped

2 tbsps tabasco sauce

½ tbsp coarsely pounded peppercorns

6 tomatoes, sliced

2 red radish, sliced

2 cucumbers, sliced

Salt

Butter

Method

1.   Wash and slice all the vegetables, avocado and mangoes and arrange in little clusters on a salver. Refrigerate.

2.   Heat butter in a skillet and add the washed and salted prawns. Grate some pepper on top of them and turn them upside down once. Add 2 tablespoons of water, cover and cook till all the prawns have become soft. Place them on the salver of vegetables.

3.   Dribble the mayonnaise on the prawns after adding the parsley and tabasco on the vegetables. Serve chilled.

Fish and Prawn Lasagne

Preparation time: 25 mins   Cooking time: 50-55 mins   Serves: 6-8

Ingredients

400 gms medium sized prawns, deveined and washed

400 gms 2" sized pomfret fillets, washed

700 gms pulped tomatoes

15 plain or spinach lasagne, boiled

6 spring onions, sliced

½ cup parsley, chopped

4 canned gherkins, chopped

3 canned pineapple slices, chopped

½ tsp mace powder

½ tsp mixed cinnamon & clove powder

½ tsp freshly grated black pepper

1 yellow pepper, cut julienne

1 red pepper, cut julienne

1 cup cheese, grated, cheddar or mozzerella

1 celery

2 tbsps tabasco sauce

Olive oil or butter

Salt

Method

1.   Salt the fish and prawns and boil separately with chopped celery.

2.   Place the pulped tomatoes in a large saucepan. Add salt, spices, peppers and celery. Allow to simmer for 20-25 minutes over a low fire. Taste for salt.

3.   Once the sauce thickens, add the cooked fish fillets and prawns, the gherkins and pineapple pieces and gently shake the pan. Allow the sauce to remain on the stove till thick. Add 3 tablespoons of butter and tabasco sauce.

4.   In a greased pyrex dish, place a third of the thick sauce at the bottom. Sprinkle with the chopped parsley and cover with a third of the lasagne noodles. Cover these with half of the remaining sauce, sprinkled with the parsley. Then layer with the remaining noodles and sauce. Sprinkle the top with parsley and grated cheese. Preheat oven to 350°F, and bake till the top is golden red. Serve directly from oven to table.

Large Tiger Prawns and Salmon Fillets with Baby Onions

Preparation time: 20 mins   Cooking time: 25-30 mins   Serves: 6-8

Ingredients

10 large tiger prawns with heads & tails, shelled and washed

8 salmon fillets, 2½" by 2½" washed

20 baby white onions

3 tbsps brown sugar

2 green cardamoms, crushed

8 green chillies, split and deseeded

1 tsp black mustard seeds

1 tbsp finely crushed garlic

1 tbsp finely crushed ginger

1 tsp red Kashmiri chilli powder

1 tsp turmeric powder

Juice of 2 to 3 sour limes

10 curry leaves

Salt

Butter

Peanut oil

Method

1.   In a large flat vessel, heat 2 tbsp each of butter and oil. Add 4 split green chillies, 5 curry leaves, ½ tsp mustard seeds and half the ginger and garlic. Stir for 2 minutes.

2.   Gently place the salted salmon fillets over the spices. Lower the flame, cover and allow to cook till tender in its own juice. Turn the fillets over once and sprinkle half the lime juice on top of them. When cooked, remove from the fire.

3.   Heat 3 tablespoons of oil in a heavy saucepan and add the remaining green chillies, mustard seeds, curry leaves, garlic and ginger, cooking for 2 minutes. Add the salted prawns. Lower heat and cook for 3 minutes. Sprinkle the chilli and turmeric powder over the prawns. Cook for another 3 minutes. Add half cup water, cover and cook till tender. Sprinkle over the lime juice. Remove from fire.

4.   Boil 2 cups water in a pan and cook the baby onions till tender. Add a pinch of salt and the brown sugar. Lower the heat and allow the onions to cook in the sticky, brown sauce till well coated. Place the heated fillets on a flat dish alongwith remaining butter gravy. Pour the prawns over them and then top with the sweet onions.

5.   Garnish the dish with lettuce leaves, cucumber, red radish and tomatoes. Serve with potato chips and toasted bread.

Spaghetti al Gamborelli with Large Prawns

Preparation time: 18 mins   Cooking time: 20 mins   Serves: 6

Ingredients

350 gms spaghetti

300 gms large prawns, shelled, deveined and washed twice

8 large cloves garlic, finely sliced

1½" ginger, finely sliced

6 green chillies, deseeded and cut julienne

250 gms tomatoes, skinned and pureed

1 tsp oregano

2 tsps paprika powder

3 spring onions, cut julienne

1 red pepper, cut julienne

1 yellow pepper, cut julienne

Salt

Olive oil

Method

1.   Boil salted water in a large pan. Add spaghetti and cook till soft. It must not be mushy. Place in cold water with a teaspoon of oil.

2.   Place 3 tablespoons of olive oil in a large skillet. Add the ginger, garlic, green chillies, oregano, paprika and the spring onions. Mix lightly and allow to cook for 5 minutes. Add the salted prawns.

3.   Cook for 7 minutes. Add the tomato pulp and the chopped bell peppers. Lower the flame and allow to cook for further 7 minutes, stirring all the time. Taste for salt.

4.   Once the prawns are soft, mix in the spaghetti, after draining the water. Stir and allow the spaghetti to assimilate the aromas of the oil, prawns, herbs and spices.

5.   Serve hot.

Daab Chingri

This is a unique Bengali dish of delicately cooked prawns in a green coconut shell. Formerly in the huge kitchens of the Bengali landowners, this prawn dish as stuffed in a coconut shell was covered with wet mud-like plaster and baked in a wood fire. All this is no longer possible in today's tiny kitchens.

However, it is possible to stuff the cooked prawns in an empty green coconut shell placed in a beautiful napkin in a large silver bowl and brought to the table to impress the guests!

Preparation time: 10 mins   Cooking time: 20 mins   Serves: 5

Ingredients

20 tiger prawns, shelled and deveined
4 medium onions, sliced
3 tbsps mustard paste, ground with a
little salt and 2 deseeded green chillies
½ large coconut, grated and ground
6 green chillies, slit
Juice of 2 sour limes

1 large green coconut
1 tsp turmeric powder
3 tsps sugar
Salt
Mustard Oil or Pure Ghee

Method

1.   Marinate the prawns in salt, turmeric powder and lemon juice for an hour.

2.   Heat ½ cup of mustard oil in a vessel over medium heat. Add the sliced onions and cook till soft. Then add the prawns and stir them for 4 minutes.

3.   Add the ground coconut, green chillies, the ground mustard and salt. Lower the heat, stir vigorously. Cover and cook for 10 minutes.

4.   Remove the lid, add sugar and keep over a low flame till the gravy has thickened.

5.   When needed, re-heat prawns gently and stuff into the empty green coconut. Bake in an oven at 350°F for 30 minutes. Serve with puris or rice.

Bengali Prawn Dolma

In Bengali, Dolma means a stuffed "Patol", a vegetable commonly known in other parts of India as "parwal". Actually, dolma is a Turkish word describing a grape leaf wrapped food package. No one knows how this word came into the Bengali language. In other parts of the world, it is known as "pointed gourd".

To make these dolmas, the outer skin is lightly scraped and a thick slice is lopped off at the top of the vegetable which is retained. With a teaspoon, remove the centre seedy portion and make a hollow to fill with stuffing. Replace the cut slice with the help of toothpicks or a flour paste.

Preparation time: 20-25 mins   Cooking time: 45 mins   Serves: 6-8

Ingredients

12 parwals, with skin scraped

300 gms shelled prawns, washed, chopped and salted

2 onions, finely chopped

3 green chillies, finely chopped

2 tsps ginger-garlic paste

1 tsp turmeric paste

1 tsp Kashmiri chilli paste

1½ tsps powdered black peppercorns, cloves and cinnamon

¼ cup fresh coriander leaves, finely chopped

6 curry leaves, finely chopped

Salt

Oil

Method

1.   Heat 2 tablespoons of oil in a pan and sauté the chopped onions. Add all the pastes, green chillies, spices and coriander and stir well.

2.   Stir the masala for 3 minutes and then add the prawns. Lower the heat and keep stirring the mixture until the prawn water has evaporated and the chopped prawns are cooked. Taste for salt.

3.   Stuff the parwals and cover them with the sliced off top as described above.

4.   Heat oil in a deep frying pan and deep fry the parwals until golden brown. Serve immediately.

Bengali Creamed Prawns — Chingri Malai Kari

Preparation time: 20 mins   Cooking time: 35 mins   Serves: 4-6

Ingredients

450 gms large prawns, deveined
Milk from 1 coconut, thick and thin
1 large onion, sliced
2 medium onions, grated to a paste
2 tsps Kashmiri chilli paste
2 tsps turmeric paste

2 tsps ginger-garlic paste
2 tsps cinnamon, cloves and cardamoms, powdered
2 tsps sugar
Salt
Pure ghee

Method

1.   Wash the prawns, salt them, and set aside.

2.   Heat 3 tablespoons of ghee in a flat-bottomed pan. Add the sliced onion and stir-fry till it is golden in colour. Set the onion aside, and in the remaining ghee, add the onion paste and cook well. Add the powdered spices, the turmeric and chilli pastes along with the fried onions and cook over a low heat.

3.   Add the salted prawns. Stir and cook for 5 minutes. Then add the sugar and the thin coconut milk. Allow the prawns to cook on low heat till the liquid evaporates.

4.   Pour in the thick coconut milk and cook till the prawns are tender. Taste for salt. Remove from the heat.

5.   Serve with a green cucumber and lettuce salad.

Bengali Creamed Prawns
(Chingri Malai Kari) ❯

Mangalorean Prawn Ghassi

Preparation time: 7-10 mins   Cooking time: 20 mins   Serves: 5-7

Ingredients

700 gms shelled, deveined prawns with
tails intact
1 large coconut, for milk
4 green chillies, split and deseeded
3 twigs curry leaves
Salt
3 tbsps refined oil

For the ground masala paste

½ small grated coconut
15 red Kashmiri chillies, deseeded and
dry roasted
3 tbsps coriander seeds, dry roasted
1 tbsp cumin seeds, dry roasted
2 tbsps cleaned tamarind

For the ground onion & chilli paste

(Roast with 2 tsps refined oil and grind)
2 large onions, coarsely chopped
2 green chillies, deseeded and chopped

Method

1.   Wash and salt the prawns and set aside in a cool place.

2.   Grind the masala till soft and buttery.

3.   Place oil in a vessel and allow to heat. Add the curry leaves and allow to crackle.
Then add the ground masala paste, lower the flame, and cook well for 5 minutes. Add
the ground onion and chilli paste, stir for 2 minutes, then add the prawns and allow to
cook over a low fire for 7 minutes.

4.   Add 1 cup of water and the split green chillies. When the mixture boils, pour in
the coconut milk. Raise the heat and bring the curry to a vigorous boil. Taste for salt.

5.   Serve piping hot with boiled rice, onion salad and papads.

*◀ Steamed Jumbo Prawns with
Garlic Butter*

Goanese Prawn Tondaak

Preparation time: 20 mins   Cooking time: 40-45 mins   Serves: 6-8

Ingredients

500 gms shelled, deveined white prawns
1 small coconut grated
3 medium sized onions, chopped finely
250 gms gram dal, soaked for 2 hours
200 gms cauliflower florets
2 tbsps tamarind pulp
2 tsps sugar
Salt
Peanut or coconut oil

For the ground masala paste
(Grind fine with a little water)
10 Kashmiri chillies, deseeded
4 green chillies, deseeded
8 large garlic cloves
1" piece crushed ginger
1½ tsps broiled coriander seeds
1 tsp broiled cumin seeds
1" piece turmeric
12 black peppercorns
2 cloves
Seeds of 1 green cardamom
1" piece cinnamon

Method

1. Wash and salt the prawns and set aside.

2. Place 3 tsps of oil in a frying pan on medium heat. Add the coconut and 2 chopped onions and mix well. Cook for 3 minutes and remove from the fire.

3. Grind the fried coconut and onions with the other masala till it is very fine.

4. Now place the remaining chopped onion in a vessel along with 2 tbsps of oil on a medium flame. Cook till soft and pink and add the salted prawns and soaked gram dal. Stir for 5 minutes, add salt and 2 cups of water and boil for 5 minutes.

5. Add the cauliflower florets and the ground masala and mix well. After 3 minutes, reduce the heat and allow to simmer till the vegetable is soft. Taste for salt. Add more water as needed. When fully cooked, add the tamarind pulp. Stir well for 3 minutes and remove from the fire.

6. Top with fresh chopped coriander leaves and serve with puris or parathas.

Saraswat Banana Bark with Prawns

This unique recipe was created by the people of Maharashtra and the Malabar coast. The bark which is the tenderest portion of the banana tree, is cooked along with prawns in a hot, spicy sauce.

This bark is sold in rolls of 12" each. Though it is not commonly available everywhere, in Mumbai it is available at the Wadala & Sion Markets.

Preparation time: 25 mins   Cooking time: 45-50 mins   Serves: 8

Ingredients

1 12" roll of tender banana bark
450 gms fresh large prawns
1 bunch spring onions, cut julienne
1 medium onion, cut into 2 and sliced
6 green chillies, deseeded and cut julienne
2" ginger, sliced and cut julienne
6 large cloves garlic, sliced and cut julienne
½ cup coriander, chopped

For the ground masala paste
(Grind fine)
1 cup grated coconut
7 Kashmiri chillies, deseeded
1 tbsp broiled coriander seeds
10 black peppercorns
½" turmeric
½ tsp cumin seeds

Juice of 2 sour limes
2 sprigs curry leaves
Salt
Peanut Oil or Ghee

Method

1. Cut the banana bark into ½" thick slices and then into small ½" pieces.

2. Boil water with salt. Add the bark pieces and the lime juice and cook for 10 minutes. Remove from fire and drain.

3. Heat 3 tablespoons of oil in a large vessel on a medium flame. Add the sliced onion and curry leaves. When the onion is lightly fried, add the bark pieces and toss for 5 minutes.

4.   Wash the prawns twice and salt them. Add them to vessel with the bark pieces. Lower the flame and cook for 5 minutes. Add ground masala and stir.

5.   Simmer for 10 minutes. Keep the vessel covered and pour water on the lid. In case you need more gravy, add more hot water on the lid. Remove from the fire after 10 minutes. Taste for salt.

6.   Heat 1 tablespoon of ghee in a non-stick frying pan. Add spring onions, green chillies, garlic and ginger and mix lightly for 3 minutes. Remove from the frying pan into a flat plate or tray. Sprinkle lightly with fine salt. Cover the cooked prawns with this mixture.

7.   When ready to serve, warm the vegetable and prawns. Serve with puris, parathas, ghee rice or khichdi, along with papads and sweet and sour pineapple chutney.

Prawns Cooked with Bread Fruit

The first time I saw a bread fruit was when my friend Indu gave me one from her garden. It is a large, knobby surfaced circular fruit twice the size of a sweet lime. The bread fruit wafers are very tasty.

Preparation time: 15 mins   Cooking time: 35-40 mins   Serves: 6-8

Ingredients

2 medium to large bread fruits, peeled and cut into pieces after removing the central core

400 gms shelled, deveined prawns

Milk of 1 coconut

½ tsp turmeric powder

½ tsp black pepper powder

2 large onions, finely chopped

Juice of 2 sour limes

2 tsps sugar

½ tsp mustard seeds

2 curry sprigs

Salt and Peanut oil

For the ground masala paste

6 green chillies, deseeded

½ cup fresh coriander leaves

1" piece ginger

4 large cloves garlic

1 tsp broiled coriander seeds

1 tsp broiled cumin seeds

1 tsp broiled sesame seeds

Method

1.   Wash the prawns, salt them and set aside.

2.   Place the onions in a vessel with 2 tablespoons of oil, curry leaves and mustard seeds and cook over a low flame. Add the ground masala and cook over a low fire for 5 to 7 minutes. Add the coconut milk, turmeric and pepper powder and boil slowly. Then add prawns and cook them till tender. Taste for salt, and remove from the fire. Mix in the lime juice and sugar.

3.   Heat oil in a frying pan and deep fry the breadfruit pieces to a golden brown. Sprinkle with fine salt and add to the prawn gravy. Serve with puris, parathas or boiled rice, and a cucumber salad or mango chutney.

Prawns Cooked with Marrows

Marrows are large cucumber type vegetables.

Preparation time: 15-20 mins   Cooking time: 25-30 mins   Serves: 6-8

Ingredients

400 gms prawns, shelled and deveined
400 gms white portion of the marrows only, cut into 1" pieces
250 gms onions, finely chopped
4 green chillies, split
2 sprigs curry leaves
½ cup tamarind pulp, thin
Salt
Sunflower oil

For the ground masala paste

(Grind fine with little water)
1 cup grated coconut
10 Begdi chillies
2" piece ginger
1 tbsp broiled coriander seeds
1 tbsp broiled poppy seeds
1 tbsp broiled sesame seeds
10 black peppercorns
1 tsp turmeric powder

Method

1.   Place the onions in a large vessel and add 3 tablespoons of oil and the curry leaves. Fry the onions till pink and soft, then add the white marrow pieces.

2.   Wash and salt the prawns and add them to the marrow. Make the flame very low, cover the vessel and add water on the lid. Allow to simmer till the marrow softens and the prawns are cooked. The marrow and prawns will both release water.

3.   Add the ground masala and the tamarind water and mix the marrow mixture gently. Pour in the hot water on the lid. Stir and taste for salt. Allow to simmer for 10 minutes and then remove from the fire.

4.   Serve with boiled rice, dry roasted Bombay Duck pieces and garlic papads or fried green chillies.

Prawn Fried Rice

Preparation time: 10 mins   Cooking time: 45 mins   Serves: 10

Ingredients

500 gms basmati rice

400 gms fresh prawns, deveined

4 tbsps soya bean sauce

5 green chillies, finely chopped

1" fresh ginger, finely chopped

20 garlic cloves, finely chopped

100 gms frenchbeans, finely chopped

100 gms carrots, finely chopped

6 spring onions, chopped diagonally

1 tbsp black pepper powder

4 eggs

2 tbsps aji-no-moto

Salt

Sesame oil

Method

1.   Wash the rice twice. Boil water in a large vessel and when it bubbles, add the rice and salt and cook till tender. Drain the rice in a colander.

2.   Wash the prawns 3 times and marinade in salt and 1 tablespoon of soya bean sauce. Set aside.

3.   Heat ½ cup of sesame oil in a wok. Add green chillies, ginger, garlic, frenchbeans, carrots, chopped spring onions and the prawns. Stir non-stop till the vegetables soften and the prawns are cooked. Remove the vegetables and prawns and wipe the wok.

4.   Pour another ½ cup of sesame oil in the wok. Put in the boiled rice and sprinkle with 3 tablespoons of the soya bean sauce. Sprinkle the rice with aji-no-moto and pepper powder. Whisk the eggs, make a hole in the rice and pour the eggs and stir fry the rice and eggs.

5.   Add the vegetable mixture with the prawns and stir the rice well on a high heat. Taste for salt. Serve the rice with sweet and sour pineapple sauce.

Prawn and Pomfret Delight

Preparation time: 30 mins   Cooking time: 55 mins   Serves: 6

Ingredients

6 pomfret fillets, skinned
24 large shelled prawns with tails intact
Juice of 2 sour limes
2 tsps black pepper powder
Rock salt
Breadcrumbs
2 egg whites

3 large potatoes, well mashed
with salt, milk and butter
Chive pieces 1½" long
½ cup parsley leaves ground
with a pinch of salt
Juice of 2 sour limes

Masala for the prawn marinade

2 tsps paprika
1 tsp turmeric powder
1 tsp coriander powder
½ tsp ginger powder

12 spinach leaves
1 yellow pepper, cut julienne
1 red pepper, cut julienne
½ kg thin frenchbeans, topped
and tailed
¼ tsp soda-bi-carb
Salt
Refined oil

Method

1. Marinate the fillets and prawns separately and set aside in a cool place.

2. Boil the potatoes and mash them fine. Add salt, butter and milk and place in a warm place.

3. Heat with ½ cup of refined oil in a non-stick frying pan. Add prawns, cover and allow to cook or shallow fry till tender. Remove when soft and place in a warm oven.

4. Whisk 2 egg whites and dip the fillets in them. Mix 1 cup of crumbs with the ground parsley and lime juice. Roll the fillets in the mixture. Add 1 cup oil in a non-stick frying pan and shallow fry the fillets.

5. Add salt and soda-bi-carb to boiling water. Add the frenchbeans and cook till tender. Drain and keep warm. Reheat the liquid and cook the spinach leaves for 5 minutes. Remove and drain the water.

6. Lightly fry the pepper strips.

7. Serve the food in individual large plates. Place a couple of spinach leaves and a few frenchbeans on them. Top with hot liquid butter. Next to it, arrange the mashed potatoes decorated with chives. Below the vegetables, place four of the large prawns and below the mashed potato, place 1 fillet of fish.

8. Serve with toasted French bread slices cut diagonally.

Prawns Baked with Beetroot and Mashed Potato

Preparation time: 25-30 mins   Cooking time: 30 mins   Serves: 8

Ingredients

For the Potatoes
900 gms potatoes, boiled and skinned
3 tbsps butter
¼ cup thick milk
1 tbsp finely chopped dill
1 tsp white pepper powder
Salt

For the Beetroot
500 gms beetroots, cooked till very tender
100 gms cream
2 medium sized onions, chopped fine
1 tsp coriander seeds, powdered
1 tsp fennel seeds, powdered
2 tsps garam masala
2 tbsps cider vinegar or wine vinegar
2 tbsps celery, finely chopped
Butter
Salt

For the Prawns
15 large prawns, shelled and deveined
1 green chilli, deseeded and chopped
2 tbsps chives, finely chopped
1 cup tomato sauce

½ tsp tabasco sauce
½ tsps crushed ginger
Butter
Salt

Methods

1. Mash the potatoes till soft, in a tray. Add the butter, milk, dill and salt. Prepare a one litre pyrex oval or rectangular dish. Place the potatoes on the bottom and sides.

2. Chop the skinned beetroots into ½" cubes.

3.   Place the butter in a saucepan and cook the onions over a medium flame till soft. Add the powdered coriander, fennel, garam masala, salt and vinegar and cook for 4 minutes. Then lightly mix the cream and beetroots, and add to the masala. Cook for 5 minutes over low heat and remove from the fire.

4.   Place the washed prawns and 2 tablespoons of butter in a saucepan with salt, ginger and ½ cup of water and cook over a low heat till soft and tender. Add the green chillies, chives, tomato sauce and tabasco sauce and cook the prawns in this mixture for 5 minutes over a low flame till well coated. Remove from the heat.

5.   Arrange the cooked beetroot in the center of the pyrex dish and arrange the prawns on top. Bake for 10-12 minutes at 350°F just before serving.

Kashmiri Ruwagon Gadh –
Fish Cooked in Tomato Gravy

Preparation time: 20 mins   Cooking time: 35-40 mins   Serves: 4-6

Ingredients

700 gms fillets of salmon or any thick white fish cut into 1½" squares, washed and salted

500 gms red tomatoes, skinned and pureed

2 cloves, very lightly crushed

1½ tsp black pepper powder

3 large black cardamoms

3 green cardamoms, crushed

1½ tsps turmeric powder

2½ tsp Kashmiri Chilli paste

1 tsp shahjeera, roughly crushed

1 tsp mace powder

2 tbsps ginger and garlic paste

1 tsp cinnamon powder

2 onions, grated

Salt

Pure ghee

Method

1.   Heat ½ cup ghee in a vessel on medium heat. When the ghee gets hot, add the green and black cardamoms, cloves, cinnamon powder and mix vigorously for 2 minutes. Add the grated onions and cook for 5 minutes and then add the tomato paste and salt and allow to come to a boil. Boil the gravy for 3 more minutes and remove from the fire. Taste for salt.

2.   Place ½ cup of ghee in a large frying pan on medium heat.

3.   Apply the chilli paste to the fish pieces which have been salted and fry them in the hot oil till golden brown. Then add the hot pieces to the gravy and serve immediately.

*Prawns baked with
Beetroot and Mashed Potato* ❯

Fried Masala Salmon

Preparation time: 25 mins   Cooking time: 25 mins   Serves: 6-8

Ingredients

1 large salmon fish, about 12" long
Salt

For the ground masala paste
(Grind in ½ cup sugarcane vinegar)
8 red Kashmiri chillies
1 tbsp cumin seeds, braised
1 tbsp coriander seeds, braised
1 tsp mustard seeds, braised
1 tsp poppy seeds, braised
2 tbsps garlic, skinned and chopped

Method

1.   Scale and wash the salmon well. Leave the head, fins and tail intact. Slit from below the mouth and remove the intestines from the stomach. Wash twice and salt the fish. Cut the skin into diamonds or squares as seen in the colour photograph facing pg. 143.

2.   Grind the masala till buttery and apply it to the fish and rub it well over the body and the stomach. Stitch up the cut or close it with toothpicks. Allow to marinade for 2 hours or overnight.

3.   Take a large iron griddle. Add enough oil to cover the whole griddle. Allow the oil to smoke and dip in the slicer which you will need to overturn the fish. If the slicer is cold, it will stick to the skin of the fish.

4.   When the oil smokes, gently lay the fish on the griddle and pour hot oil from the griddle onto it. Baste with the hot oil till the lower side is cooked and golden brown. Then turn over gently without breaking the head or tail. Serve on a tray covered with greens.

❮ *Top: Fried Surmai Slice*
Below: Fried Masala Salmon

Salmon Cutlets in Butter

Preparation time: 8 mins   Cooking time: 16-20 mins   Serves: 6

Ingredients

9 large slices of salmon or ghol fish
Parsley sprigs
1½ tsp black pepper
2 tsps green chilli juice, fresh and
strained from a fine sieve

Sour lime slices
300 gms butter
3 tbsps peanut oil

Method

1.   Wash the thick fish slices gently. Salt them and apply black pepper powder and the green chilli juice and allow to stand for 30 minutes.

2.   Just before serving the fish, place butter and peanut oil in a large non-stick pan and heat over a medium flame.

3.   When hot, fry the fish slices gently, three at a time, covering them for 5 minutes on each side. Then cook them uncovered till golden brown.

4.   Place them on a flat dish and top with the left-over butter-oil gravy. Garnish with parsley sprigs.

5.   Serve with hot, fluffy, mashed potatoes.

Italian Fish Stew

Ingredients

500 gms filleted pieces of kingfish, salmon, ghol or pomfrets

500 gms mussels with shells, cleaned and washed

250 gms small squid hoods, cut into rings

6 spring onions, 6" from roots upwards, sliced

800 gms fresh tomatoes, pulped

½ cup tomato sauce

1 cup dry white wine

2 litres fish stock (see pg. 2)

8 large cloves, crushed

2 tbsps fresh ginger, grated

3 green chillies, deseeded and chopped fine

3 sprigs fresh thyme

½ cup fresh parsley, chopped

1½ tsp sweet red pepper powder

Black pepper, freshly grated

1 tbsp sugar

1 large pinch saffron strands

¼ cup olive oil

Salt

Method

1.   Heat the saffron on an iron griddle. Allow to heat gently and crumble.

2.   Heat oil in a heavy saucepan over a medium flame and add the sliced onion, garlic, thyme, green chillies, ginger, sweet red pepper powder, black pepper and salt. Mix lightly and cook for 5 minutes. Add the tomato pulp with the sugar. Stir and simmer for 20 minutes.

3.   Pour the fish stock into the saucepan. Add the wine and simmer for 20-25 minutes. Add the salted fish and cook for 10 minutes. Then add the mussels.

4.   Boil squid rings separately for 45 minutes and then add to the stew. Taste for salt and add the black pepper and the sweet red pepper.

5.   When the stew boils, sprinkle the crumbled saffron. Add tomato sauce and stir for 5 minutes. Sprinkle with parsley and serve hot with toasted bread.

Creamed Salmon Served on Toasted Bread Roundels

Preparation time: 20 mins   Cooking time: nil   Serves: 12

Ingredients

24 round pieces of bread, cut from slices of brown or white bread

700 gms salmon, boiled, skinned and deboned

200 gms cream

200 gms soft cream cheese

1 tsp black pepper powder

1 tsp tabasco sauce

Juice of 3 sour limes

Salt

Butter

Method

1.   Place the salmon in a large round bowl and mash well. Gradually, whilst mashing, add the pepper powder and tabasco sauce and lastly mix in the cream, and the cream cheese. Taste for salt. Chill.

2.   When ready to serve, toast the bread roundels and butter them and pipe them with the salmon mixture.

3.   Garnish with sprigs of parsley and spring onions.

4.   Serve with chilled white wine.

Large Fish and Potato Puff Soufflé

Preparation time: 15 mins   Cooking time: 55-60 mins   Serves: 6-8

Ingredients

For the Bake:

500 gms ghol, seer, salmon, pomfret or any other fish, boiled and flaked

250 gms finely mashed potatoes – add salt and a little cream

Juice of 2 sour lime juice

3 tbsps celery

3 tbsps onion, finely chopped

Black pepper

3 eggs, separated

Salt

Butter

For the Sauce:

½ litre milk

3 hard boiled eggs, finely chopped

2 tbsps butter

2½ tbsps fine flour

Method

To make the Sauce:

1.   Heat butter in a saucepan over a moderate flame. Add the flour and stir vigorously. Do not allow the mixture to brown. Remove from the fire when ivory coloured and add the milk and salt and stir well.

2.   Replace over a moderate flame and stir continuously until smooth sauce with a satin finish.

3.   Add the chopped boiled eggs and a little tabasco sauce, if liked.

For the Fish Bake:

1.   Place 2 tablespoons of butter in a saucepan. When hot, add the onions and cook till soft. Add the parsley, 3 beaten egg yolks, lime juice, mashed potatoes and the boiled fish. Mix well. Add salt and pepper to taste. Fold in 3 stiffly beaten egg whites.

2.   Pour the mixture into a greased soufflé dish and place in a heated oven at 400°F for 40 minutes.

3.   Serve with the sauce.

Turkish Baked Whole Fish

Preparation time: 25 mins   Cooking time: 1 hr. 20 mins   Serves: 6

Ingredients

1 large fish salmon or mullet about 1½ kg

3 large potatoes, skinned and sliced into ¼" thickness

4-5 carrots, cleaned and cut into slices

1 green capsicum, deseeded and cut julienne

1 golden pepper, deseeded and cut julienne

2 medium onions, cut into half and then cut into slightly thick square pieces

8-10 large cloves garlic

½ cup tomato sauce or ketchup

1 tsp cumin seeds, braised

1 tsp coriander seeds, braised

1 tsp black pepper, freshly grated

1 tsp sweet red chillies, freshly ground

3 very thick stalks of parsley cut into ½" thick rings

Salt

Olive oil

Parsley sprigs for garnishing

1 large lemon, sliced

Method

1.   Wash the vegetables and drain them. Clean and wash the fish.

2.   Heat ¾ cup olive oil in a large pan with a lid. Add the vegetables, sprinkled with salt and cook covered for about 25-35 minutes till the vegetables are soft.

3.   Place the fish in a large pyrex dish. Arrange the cooked vegetables around it. Taste for salt.

4.   Slice the garlic and fry it in the remaining vegetable oil. Then add the tomato sauce, chilli powder, pepper powder, cumin and coriander seeds. Stir well and add one litre of water to the hot sauce and then pour all the liquid over the fish and the vegetables.

5.   Bake the fish in an oven at 350°F for 45-55 minutes.

6.   Serve the fish garnished with parsley sprigs and lemon slices.

Indian Salmon Curry

Preparation time: 15 mins   Cooking time: 20 mins   Serves: 8

Ingredients

10 medium slices of salmon
1 medium sized coconut, grated and
divided into 2 portions
2 medium onions, finely chopped
8 large garlic cloves
1 tbsp coriander seeds, braised

7 peppercorns
8 red Kashmiri chillies
1½" fresh turmeric piece
½ cup fresh coriander leaves, chopped
Salt
Oil

Method

1.   Remove milk from one portion of the grated coconut.

2.   Grind together one portion of the coconut with one onion, garlic, coriander seeds, turmeric, red chillies and a little water to a fine paste.

3.   Place 3 tablespoons oil in a vessel. Add 1 chopped onion and place on medium heat. When the onion is soft and pink, put in the ground paste. Stir and allow to cook for 4 minutes. Then add the coconut milk and allow to simmer for 5 minutes. Taste for salt.

4.   Now add the fish and the tamarind pulp and shake the vessel with both hands. Sprinkle the chopped coriander on top of the fish gravy.

5.   Simmer for 7 more minutes and serve with boiled rice and papads.

Salmon Fish à La Bombay

Preparation time: 28 mins   Cooking time: 45 mins   Serves: 6-8

Ingredients

8 medium sized salmon fillets, skin removed

2 tbsps chives cut

6 potatoes, boiled, skinned and mashed

¼ cup cream

1 cup cheddar cheese or any other strong cheese, grated

2 egg yolks

½ litre white sauce, with chopped parsley

100 gms sliced mushrooms

½ cup breadcrumbs tossed in ¼ cup melted butter

Black pepper, freshly ground

Salt

Butter

Method

1.   Marinate the salmon fillets in salt and pepper for an hour.

2.   Mash the potatoes. Add fine salt and black pepper.

3.   Grease an oval baking dish and line its sides and bottom with the potato.

4.   Place the white sauce in a saucepan. Beat in the egg yolks and add the grated cheese and pour half the quantity over the mashed potatoes.

5.   Place the salmon fillets neatly over the white sauce. Sprinkle with the chives.

6.   Cover the fish with the remaining sauce. Top with the buttered breadcrumbs and bake at 350°F in an oven till golden red.

7.   Serve with a green salad.

Salmon Fillets Cooked in Saffron Sauce

Preparation time: 15-20 mins   Cooking time: 20-25 mins   Serves: 6

Ingredients

8 thick salmon fish fillets
1 coconut, milk removed
1 gm saffron
1 tsp chilli powder
1 tbsp black peppercorns
2 tbsps garlic, sliced
1 green chilli, finely chopped

1 large onion, finely chopped
1 tbsp rice flour
2 tbsps coriander, chopped
Mint sprigs
Salt
Butter

Method

1.   Wash the fish fillets and marinate in salt and set aside.

2.   Heat the saffron and crumble into 1 cup of hot water and allow to steep. Keep the milk of one coconut in a cool place.

3.   Fry the onions in 3 tablespoons butter. Add the green chilli and garlic slices. Cook till soft. Mix the rice flour in ½ cup of water and add it along with the coconut milk and the steeped saffron. Lower the flame and cook for 10 minutes till the gravy thickens. Taste for salt.

4.   Take a thick paper bag and place the peppercorns in it and pound with a heavy pestle. Sprinkle the fish with chilli powder and roll in the crushed peppercorns.

5.   Heat 3 or more tablespoons of butter and fry the fish fillets over medium heat till both sides turn brown. Remove on a flat dish and pour over the saffron sauce.

Barbecued Salmon

Preparation time: 10 mins   Cooking time: 25 mins   Serves: 6-8

Ingredients

1 large salmon, about 2-2½ kgs
2 large whole garlic cloves, separated
½ cup parsley
2 tbsps sage
1 tbsp coarsely crushed coriander seeds
1½ tbsps coarsely crushed cumin seeds

2 onions, finely minced
Juice of 3 sour limes
1 tsp black peppercorns, coarsely ground
Lettuce leaves or banana leaves
Olive oil or Sunflower oil

Method

1.   Start the coals burning in the barbeque.

2.   Wash and scale the fish thoroughly. Keep the head intact. Remove fins and sides and leave the tail. Scrub well and wash the large stomach thoroughly. Salt the fish and keep it in a cool place.

3.   Crush the skinned garlic cloves and mix them with the minced onions, parsley, sage, lime juice, ground cumin seeds, ground coriander seeds and the peppercorns. Place in a bowl and add 4 tablespoons of olive oil or sunflower oil.

4.   Make diagonal cuts on both sides of the fish and smear it well with the oil mixture. Allow to marinate for 2 hours.

5.   Wrap the fish with lettuce leaves or in tender banana leaves with the center stalk removed. Tie the whole fish like a parcel with a string. Pierce it in 3 places, near the tail, centre and below the head by thin iron rods or seeks.

6.   When the coals are red, place the fish on top of the grid and turn gently so that the fish does not get charred. Baste with oil. The leaves may char, but the fish will get cooked within 15-25 minutes, depending upon its thickness.

7.   Place the fish in a flat dish, remove the leaves and eat immediately to enjoy the aroma of the leaves that the coals have imparted to the fish.

8.   Serve with a green salad and hot, long French bread.

Meen Yevichathu from Kerala

Preparation time: 22 mins   Cooking time: 15-20 mins   Serves: 4-6

Ingredients

400 gms of 2" x 2" fish pieces of
salmon, kingfish, pomfret, ghol
or any other fish, washed twice
3 medium sized onions, chopped fine
2 split green chillies
5 pieces kokum, washed
1 sprig curry leaves
Salt
3 tbsps peanut oil

For the ground masala paste
(Grind fine with a little water)
 8-10 Reshampatti chillies
10 large cloves garlic
1½" piece fresh ginger, cleaned
1" piece turmeric, fresh or dry
1 tbsp cumin seeds
1 tsp fenugreek seeds
½ tsp mustard seeds

Method

1.   Place the oil in a large vessel and put it on a medium flame.

2.   Salt the fish pieces.

3.   When the oil gets hot, add the mustard seeds, chopped onions, and the masala and mix vigorously for 5 minutes. Add 2½ cups of water and allow the mixture to come to a boil. Add the fish pieces, the kokum, the slit chillies and the curry sprigs. Lower the flame. Allow to simmer till cooked. Taste for salt.

4.   Serve hot with boiled rice and a green vegetable like frenchbeans.

Salmon Fillets in Lemon-Butter

Preparation time: 15 mins   Cooking time: 20 mins   Serves: 6

Ingredients

For the fillets

8 salmon fillets, with skin removed
Juice of 2 sour limes
1 tsp black pepper powder
1 tbsp ginger juice
Salt
Butter

2 cups mayonnaise (see recipe on pg. 2)
Lettuce leaves
1 red pepper, chopped
2 tbsps dill leaves, chopped
into ½" pieces

Method

1.   Wash the fillets twice. Salt and set aside.

2.   Heat 2 cups of water in a flat-bottomed vessel. Add a pinch of salt, pepper powder, lime juice, ginger juice and 3 tablespoons of butter. When the liquid boils, slip in the fillets. Cover and cook till tender. Remove from the fire and place the fish in a flat dish along with any lime and butter gravy which remains. Chill.

3.   Serve with chilled mayonnaise along with red pepper, dill and some Oak leaf salad.

Steamed Baby Salmon with Hollandaise Sauce

Preparation time: 10 mins   Cooking time: 18 mins   Serves: 4

Ingredients

2 baby salmon, about 8" long
1 small onion, sliced
20 coriander seeds, broiled
1 tbsp black pepper powder
Juice of 2 sour limes

Parsley
4 green chillies, slit, deseeded
1 portion Hollandaise sauce (see recipe on pg. 5)
Salt
2 tbsp butter

Method

1.   Keep the salmon whole. Remove the gills and make a small cut near the stomach to remove the entrails. Scale the fish. Keep the fins and tail. Wash thoroughly.

2.   Marinade in salt, pepper powder and lime juice for 2 hours. Turn the fish every 30 minutes.

3.   Take a long, flat vessel and pour enough water to cover the fish. Add parsley, sliced onion, green chillies, coriander seeds, butter and a pinch of salt. Allow to boil for 5 minutes.

4.   Drain and place on a silver salver decorated with endive lettuce, tomatoes, cucumber and beetroots. Cover with the Hollandaise sauce and serve.

Salmon Pulao

This is one of my favourite fish dishes. I must stress, though, the importance of using fresh fish while preparing the pulao.

Preparation time: 20-25 mins   Cooking time: 1 hr   Serves: 6-8

For the Fish Stock:

2 kgs salmon fillets
1 onion, chopped
1 potato, peeled and chopped
2 tomotoes, skinned and diced
5 celery pieces, 3" each
½" ginger, sliced

2 Kashmiri chillies, deseeded
4 sprigs parsley, chopped
2 pieces lemon grass
Salt

1.   Take a large salmon, atleast weighing 2 kgs. Cut it into 3 pieces, a large head, a large stomach and a small tail piece (which can be used to make cutlets or steaks). Clean the head and cut it up for making a stock. Cut the stomach into 2 long pieces and throw away the intestines. Debone and remove the skin and cut the flesh into 1½" squares.

2.   Wash the head and bones well and put them in a large vessel with 7 cups of water. Add onion, potato, tomatoes, celery pieces, ginger, Kashmiri chillies and coarse salt.

3.   Add parsley sprigs, lemon grass bruised lightly, and salt.

4.   Boil for 40-45 minutes, till you get a thick stock. Strain the stock through a fine sieve and discard the bones and vegetables.

For the Fish:

500 gms salmon fish,
cut into 1½" fillets

1½ tsps ground black pepper
Rock salt

1.   Wash and marinate the fish in salt, lime juice and black pepper powder.

For the Fish Masala:

7 deseeded Kashmiri chillies, soaked overnight, in sugarcane vinegar
1" fresh ginger, sliced
6 large cloves garlic
½ tsp green cardamom seeds

10 black peppercorns
½" cinnamon
4 mace flowers
1 star anise

1.   Apply the ground masala to the marinated fish.

2.   Heat a frying pan with sunflower oil. When hot, lightly fry the fillets in small batches. Drain on paper towels. Set aside.

For the Risotto (Rice):

750 gms long grained basmati rice
2 large onions, finely sliced
3 bay leaves
10 black peppercorns, lightly crushed
3 mace flowers
2 pieces ½" cinnamon

As much fish stock as necessary to cook the rice and fish
1 gm saffron, heated lightly on a griddle and mixed into ½ cup of hot water
Salt
3 tbsps pure ghee

1.   Fry the sliced onions in pure ghee until light golden in colour and add the bay leaves, peppercorns, mace and cinnamon and fry for 2 minutes. Then add the rice, washed twice, and lower the heat and stir for 5 minutes. Empty this out into an electric cooker along with sufficient water. If no cooker is available, carry on in the same vessel.

2.   Add the saffron water.

3.   Add sufficient strained stock to cook the rice as well as fish and add any fish masala that remains after applying to the fish fillets.

4.   Bring to a boil in the electric cooker or vessel and then add the fish pieces. Cover and cook till the rice is soft and tender.

5.   Empty out onto a silver salver and garnish with green lettuce leaves, deep fried slices of almonds and raisins.

Cold Salmon Mousse

Preparation time: 40 mins   Cooking time: 30 mins   Serves: 8-10

Ingredients

500 gms flaked fish, boiled and boned
100 gms cream, whipped
3 tbsps gelatine
2 tbsps red wine (optional)
1 tbsp black pepper, freshly ground
2 cups boiled fish stock or chicken clear soup
2½ cups milk
2 bay leaves
¾ cup self-raising flour
1 stalk celery
1 small carrot

2 single spring onions
¼ tsp nutmeg
1 small piece of fresh ginger
2 small packets of butter
2 green chillies, deseeded
1 tbsp tabasco or capsico sauce
Canned pineapple slices and cherries for garnish
Juice of 2 sour limes
1 star anise or badian
Salt

Method

1.   Cut the salmon in slices after removing the scales. Cut up the head and tail. Remove the gills and intestines from the fish and wash the head, tail, and all the sliced pieces twice under running water. Salt the fish and marinate in sour lime juice.

2.   Place the fish in a large vessel along with 6 cups of water and salt, a few whole black peppercorns, star anise, sliced spring onions, 1 sliced carrot, coarsely chopped stalk of celery and a small piece of ginger cut into strips. Bring to a boil and cook the fish in open vessel till it is tender and soft.

3.   Then drain the soup and set aside and if you wish, use it instead of the chicken soup. Flake the fish and throw away all the skin and bones. We will need 500 gms of the white boiled fish.

Top: Spaghetti al Gamborelli
Below: Salmon Pulao ❯

4.   Take 2½ cups of creamy milk and heat it in a saucepan. In another saucepan, heat 1 small packet butter and fry the flour in it over a very low flame. Stir for 2 minutes and pour in the hot milk and stir non-stop till you get a smooth white sauce. Add salt.

5.   Blend the fish and green chopped chillies in a mixer-grinder along with ½ cup of the reserved fish soup. Taste the mixture for salt. Add to the white sauce.

6.   Slowly mix in the black pepper, wine, tabasco sauce and cream with the fish. The cream should be very lightly beaten.

7.   Take 1 tablespoon of gelatine and melt it in ½ cup of fish soup till it dissolves. Cool. Chill for ½ hour. When it starts to thicken, pour it into the fish mixture. Pour the fish in a glass bowl and even out the surface with a spatula. Chill.

8.   Boil the rest of the gelatine in a saucepan with 1 cup of fish soup. Set aside.

9.   Garnish the top of the mousse with a nice arrangement of the pineapple slices and cherries, and pour the gelatine evenly over the surface of the bowl. Cover with foil and chill overnight.

10. You can garnish in any other way, if you wish. I like to use finely sliced carrots made into flowers over a base of mashed potato with tomato roses and green leaves made from the tops of spring onions.

11. Serve accompanied by thick slices of chilled, ripe, skinned Alphonso mangoes and lettuce leaves.

‹ *Spicy Sardines*

Sardines

The sardine is a slender fish, with an elongated body. Its back is bluish green and abdomen silver coloured with a pink tinge. Its Hindi and Marathi name is Tarli. This fish was abundantly found off the coast of Sardinia and it got its name from this island.

This small fish is very important for us humans because it contains Omega-3 fatty acids, protein and calcium. Sardines are cold water fish and contain the highest amount of Omega-3 fatty acids when compared to other fish. It is rich in phosphorus, iron, potassium, Vitamin B76 and Niacin.

Napoleon Bonaparte in the beginning of the 19th century, realized that there was great need to preserve foods and the sardine was the first fish to be preserved in oil or tomato sauce. It is one of the world's first canned foods. The most famous sardines are the ones canned in Portugal.

It is also known as the Atlantic or sea herring or as "pilchards". There are more than 20 species of this salt water fish. In the U.S. the sardines are actually herring.

Sardines are a great favourite of people living in the state of Kerala in India.

Because of easy availability of ice and quick transport facilities, a large amount of the oil sardine catch is now eaten in fresh condition. A major portion of the catch is cured with salt and sun dried during the glut period.

The sardine canning industry in India has suffered many setbacks from time to time because of technical and practical difficulties. At present this canning industry has revived in Kerala and private factories for canning sardines have been set up in Cochin, Calicut and Alleppey. Due to the high price, canned sardines are not sold easily in the local markets.

Stuffed Sprats or Large Sardines

Preparation time: 30 mins   Cooking time: 30 mins   Serves: 6-8

Ingredients

18 large sprats
400 gms cream cheese
1 tbsp fresh ginger, crushed
1 tbsp fresh garlic, crushed
2 tbsps green chillies, deseeded and
finely chopped
½ tsp black pepper powder

Juice of 4 sour limes
1½ tsps turmeric powder
2 tsps red chilli powder
3-4 beaten eggs
Breadcrumbs
Salt
Peanut oil

Method

1.   Wash the sprats. Scale them after removing their heads.

2.   Slit each small fish from the stomach side with a very sharp, small knife. Remove the backbone. Wash the fish thoroughly and spread on a tray.

3.   Apply salt, turmeric and chilli powder to the sprats and sprinkle the lime juice over them.

4.   Place the cream cheese in a large glass bowl. Gently mix in the ginger, garlic, green chillies and pepper powder. Then stuff the sprats with this mixture.

5.   Place a large frying pan on the fire with the peanut oil.

6.   When the oil gets hot, dip the fish in the beaten egg, roll them in the breadcrumbs and deep fry till golden red.

7.   Serve with lashings of mayonnaise, a green salad with lemon dressing and finger chips.

Spicy Sardines

These sardines can be eaten as a pickle.

Preparation time: 15-20 mins   Cooking time: 25-30 mins   Serves: 4-6

Ingredients

450 gms sardines
4 medium sized onions, sliced
8 large cloves garlic, sliced
2" ginger, sliced and cut into thin strips
1-1½ cup sugarcane vinegar
3 sprigs curry leaves
Salt
Sesame or peanut oil

For the ground masala paste
(Grind fine in a little vinegar)
8 Reshampatti chillies, deseeded
1 cup coconut, grated
2 tsps turmeric powder
2 tsps cumin seeds
1 tsp fenugreek seeds
½ cup fresh coriander leaves
2 green chillies, deseeded

Method

1.   Clean the sardines thoroughly, removing their guts. Wash the stomach portions well. Leave whole. Salt them.

2.   Take 1 cup of oil and place it in a flat, thick-bottomed vessel over medium heat. When the oil gets hot, add the curry leaves and the onions. Cook for 5 minutes, after which add the garlic and ginger, lower the flame and allow the onions to cook till golden and soft.

3.   Mix the sardines with the ground masala paste until coated. Then slowly place them on the cooked sliced onions. Shake the pan with both hands. Pour 1 cup vinegar over the sardines and cook on a very low fire till soft. Taste for salt and remove the vessel from the stove.

4.   Store in a glass or stainless steel container with a tight lid.

Kerala Type Dried Sardines

Traditionally, most fish is cooked in terracotta flat-bottomed, high sided vessels. However, an aluminium vessel can also be used to make this simple dish.

Preparation time: 18 mins   Cooking time: 25-35 mins   Serves: 6-8

Ingredients

35 small sardines, scaled,
cleaned and washed
8 curry leaves
Salt
½ to ¾ cup coconut or peanut oil

For the ground masala paste
(Grind coarsely with a little water)
12 Reshampatti chillies, deseeded
4 long green chillies, deseeded
15 large garlic cloves
2" piece fresh ginger
2" piece fresh or dried turmeric
1 tbsp cumin seeds
10 black peppercorns
Seeds of 3 green cardamoms
5 pieces of kokum or green mangoes

Method

1. Make a tiny cut on each side of the sardine. Salt and set aside.

2. Mix the ground masala with the oil and a little fine salt.

3. Grease the terracotta or aluminium vessel.

4. Place layers of sardines interspersed with the ground masala paste until all are used up. Sprinkle 1½ cups of water over the fish. Cover tightly with foil as well as a lid and place over a low fire till the sardines are cooked.

5. Serve hot with sambhar, rice and papads.

Sardines Baked in Tomato and Lime Juice

Preparation time: 24 mins   Cooking time: 20-30 mins   Serves: 6

Ingredients

12 large fresh sardines
5 tomatoes, skinned and thickly sliced
Juice of 4 sour limes
1 tbsp fresh or dried oregano, chopped
½ cup parsley or coriander leaves, chopped,
Salt
Olive oil

For the ground masala paste
(Grind Fine)
7 black peppercorns
6 green chillies, deseeded
12 large cloves garlic
2 tsps broiled, cumin seed

Method

1.   Wash the sardines and place them on a wooden board. Cut off the heads and remove the entrails from the stomach. Slice down the cut side of the stomach to the tail with a thin, sharp knife and remove backbone. Wash the sardine and lay flat on its unskinned stomach side. Press heavily with the bottom of your hand to flatten it out.

2.   When sardines are ready, sprinkle them with the lime juice. Apply the ground chilli mixture and salt and marinade well. Leave for 30 minutes.

3.   Take a large baking dish or tray. Grease it heavily with olive oil.

4.   Lay the slices of tomatoes on the greased tray. Sprinkle lightly with salt and oregano. Then lay the marinated sardines on top of the tomatoes. The skin side should be on top. Sprinkle with chopped parsley or coriander.

5.   Heat the oven to 350°F. Drizzle ½ cup of olive oil over the fish and allow to bake for 15-20 minutes, till tender.

6.   Serve with hot toast and tomato chutney.

Silver Barfish cooked in Black Gram and Fenugreek

Preparation time: 10-12 mins   Cooking time: 15 mins   Serves: 4-6

Ingredients

1 silver barfish, washed and salted
2 onions, finely chopped
½ large coconut, grated divided
in 2 portions

For the Tadka:

½ tsp split black gram
¼ tsp fenugreek seeds
½ cup coriander, finely chopped
Salt
Oil

For the ground masala paste

(Grind together)
1 onion
½ coconut
2 tsps braised coriander seeds
¾ tsp turmeric powder
8 red Kashmiri chillies
8 peppercorns
1 tsp raw rice
1 tsp split black gram
½ tsp fenugreek seeds
1 tbsp tamarind pulp

Method

1.   Grind one onion with the chillies, turmeric, black gram, rice, coconut, fenugreek seeds and peppercorns into a very fine paste.

2.   In a frying pan, add 2 tablespoons of oil and when hot, add the black gram and fenugreek seeds. When they splutter, add the finely chopped onions and cook till soft. Add the coconut, chilli masala to the pan and stir for a few minutes.

3.   Cut the silver barfish into pieces. Wash. Add to the masala and stir gently. Then add the grated coconut. Allow the fish to simmer in the masala till soft. If necessary, add ½ cup of water.

4.   Sprinkle with chopped coriander and serve hot.

The Flat Fishes – Sole, Turbot

Flat fish contain less fat and are good for quick drying and preservation.

The flat fishes have compressed bodies and the eyes are on the left or right side of the head. The side on which the eyes are situated, is always coloured, whereas the blind side is pale white. The scales of the 2 sides are also different. These fishes have the capacity to change their body colour to match with their surroundings.

The sea fish include those which live in the bottom and have burrowing habits, such as flounders, halibuts, tongue-soles and soles. The sole fishery is very important along the coast of Malabar in India, and is only next to the oil sardine, mackerel and prawn fisheries.

Over 90 species of flat fish belonging to the group Heterostomata have been recorded from Indian waters and are grouped into 7 families.

One important fish is the Malabar sole or tongue-sole known in Marathi as "Lepti" or "Shivra". It is commonly known as "Zipti".

Fillets de Sole Bonne Femme

Preparation time: 15 mins   Cooking time: 50-55 mins   Serves: 8

Ingredients

8-12 fillets of sole or if unavailable,
pomfrets
500 gms button mushrooms
6 spring onions, sliced 6" from
root to green
1 cup white wine
Black pepper, freshly grated
Juice of 2 sour limes
Salt
2½ tbsps olive oil or any other oil

For the Sauce:
400 gms butter
150 gms flour or self-raising flour
400 gms cream
White pepper, ground
Parsley, chopped
Salt

Method

1.   Wash and clean the mushrooms. Separate the caps of 16 mushrooms and set them aside. Slice the rest of the mushrooms along with their stalks.

2.   Marinade the fillets in salt, pepper and the lime juice for 20 minutes.

3.   Grease a large flat pan and place the fillets in a line at the bottom. Pour the wine over the fillets and sufficient water to cover them. If all the fillets don't fit a single file, stack them, one on top of the other. Place the dish on a low fire and allow the fish to simmer until cooked but still firm. Remove any liquid in the dish into a saucepan and heat it to reduce to 1 cup. Heat butter and a little oil in a non-stick frying pan and cook the tops of the mushrooms and sliced mushrooms separately and set aside.

4.   Heat 200 grams butter in a large saucepan. Add the flour and stir well. Remove from fire and stir in the poaching liquid. Add the sliced mushrooms. Return to medium heat and stir non-stop until the sauce boils. Add ½ cup of cream and stir. Gradually add the cream. Add salt and pepper and remove from the fire. Stir in the lime juice. Add all the butter, whisking it in a little at a time.

5.   Slowly and gently pour the sauce over the fillets. Sprinkle with the chopped parsley. Decorate with the mushroom caps. Serve hot.

Sole Fish Cooked in Butter and Coriander

Preparation time: 7 mins   Cooking time: 15 mins   Serves: 4

Ingredients

1 large sole fish, cleaned and cut into slices.
½ tsp mustard seeds
6 spring onions, cut julienne
6 long green chillies, cut julienne

1½" of ginger, cut julienne
6 large garlic cloves, cut julienne
2 tbsps coriander, chopped
Salt
Butter

Method

1.   Wash and salt the fish slices, and set aside. Discard head and fins.

2.   Place 200 gms butter in a large flat-bottomed vessel on medium flame.

3.   When the butter begins to melt, add the mustard seeds, spring onions, chillies, and garlic. Stir for 3 minutes and add the fish slices. Lower the flame, cover the vessel and cook one side for 5 minutes. Then turn over and cook the other side for 5 minutes.

4.   Remove to a flat dish whilst hot, pouring the butter sauce over the fish.

5.   Sprinkle coriander and serve with potato chips and a green salad.

On Squids and Octopus

People love to go to Chinese Restaurants to eat deep fried, crispy, squid rings. But they know nothing about the squid as a fish. Here is some enthralling information on it.

All squids have 10 arms, making them decapods. Octopus has 8 arms. Eight of the squid's arms are of the same size. Two longer arms are called tentacles. In almost all the species the tentacles have "clubs", flattened expanded appendages at the end of the tentacles. These clubs often have wicked hooks and claws in the suckers which only appear on the flattened ends.

Squids are carnivorous. They eat fish, crustaceans, shell fish and worms. Squids catch their prey by grabbing it with the two tentacles. These are usually held close to their bodies in pouchlike sacs. They shoot out like harpoons, grab the prey and pull it into their circle of arms.

Many squids have poison glands with which they inject neurotoxins into the prey. This done, the horny beak chops the prey into bite-size pieces. These go down the throat into its stomach.

Squids and Octopus are fish that have reached the ultimate in invertebrate evolution. They are known as CEPHALOPODS and have a highly advanced nervous system. They have other evolutionary features also, which give them great advantage in the sea. Their fast ability to "change colours and body patterns gives them easy camouflage, helps them to escape fast, and helps in mating and communication."

Squids and octopus are compared to humans without bones. They have human-like eyes. The squids have a shell called the PEN. This is internal and runs along the squid's back to keep its body stiff.

Squids and octopus have the largest brains of any invertebrates. They have the ability to sense and process environmental information which puts them on a level, the same as many fishes. The learning ability of an octopus shows that its intelligence has been compared to "canine babies".

Squids belong to a type of category of organisms called nekton. These have developed the powers of motion to propel themselves against ocean currents.

There are about 500 types of squid, from pygmy size upto a colossal size.

At the time of mating male squids flash their signals. If a female likes a pattern, they will both embrace by intertwining their arms. Sperm will emerge from the male's funnel which he will catch with one of his arms and place in a pocket beneath the she's mouth. The she squid will release her eggs and hold them in her arms. She triggers the packets of sperms to open and fertilizes the eggs. In the frenzy of copulation, the rigours of mating weakens the squid. Those who do not die are eaten up by the numerous sea lions, sharks and dolphins who come to watch the 'tamasha'. One female squid will lay millions of eggs. The jelly-like substance which surrounds them is not palatable to other sea life so they are safe until they hatch.

The squid brain is made up of two 'fused' nerve centers. These are linked down the length of the body by 2 giant nerve axons. These axons are bundles of fused nerves that transmit nerve signals to help the squid escape danger.

Squids have eyes very much like humans. Their retinas are made up of rods and cones. They also have an eyelid. Each squid eye can focus separately. The big optic nerve feeds into the brain for processing information. "Rapid fire nerve fibers" allow them to respond fast.

The squid escapes its enemies by spurting black ink which for a time confuses its enemy and allows it to escape. One species of squid spends its life in darkness under the sea. It 'ejects' a cloud of light bacteria or luminescence so that its enemy might be temporarily blinded.

The squids' nervous control of their circulatory system allows them to create athletic feats. Their use of colour implies a kind of language between them. They use "arm signals". If upraised, the arm means "go away". It is possible that schools of squids give out a signal before an attack.

Out of all the invertebrates in the ocean, the squids and the octopus are the most fascinating.

Calamari or Squid – Italian Style

Ingredients

1 kg squid rings
2 large onions, finely chopped
6 green chillies, deseeded and finely chopped
2" ginger, finely crushed
8 cloves garlic, finely sliced
2 cups fresh tomato pulp

3 bay leaves
1 tbsp fresh marjoram or 1 tsp dry
2 tsps red chilli powder
1 tsp black pepper powder
2 cups red wine
Salt
Olive oil

Method

1.   Cut the squid into ¼" thick rings. Wash twice, salt and set aside.

2.   In a large thick-bottomed pan, pour ½ cup of oil and place on a medium flame. When the oil heats up, add the squid rings and sauté lightly for 5 minutes. Then add the finely chopped onions, ginger, garlic and green chillies. Stir well for another 5 minutes.

3.   Add the bay leaves, marjoram, chilli and black pepper powders. Stir well, add 4 cups of water and allow to cook for 1¼ hours until the squid gets cooked.

4.   If the water should dry up, add a little more at a time.

5.   When the squid is cooked, add the tomato pulp and red wine. Simmer for 10 minutes and serve hot with French bread or crisp bread with a lettuce and cucumber salad.

Calamares Rellinos or Spanish Style Stuffed Squids

Preparation time: 45 mins   Cooking time: 1½ hrs.   Serves: 6-8

Ingredients

12 fairly large squid hoods at least 5-6" in height

700 gms skinned and finely chopped tomatoes

3 cups boiled basmati rice

2 brown onions, cut into halves and thinly sliced into half moons

10 large cloves garlic

6 green chillies, deseeded and chopped fine

1½" fresh ginger, skinned and grated

½ cup parsley, freshly chopped

200 gms ham, finely chopped into tiny cubes

1 tbsp sweet red chilli powder

1 tsp black pepper, freshly grated

¼ cup tomato sauce

1 tbsp sugar

¾ cup white wine

Salt

Olive oil

Method

1. Wash the fish hoods well.

2. Heat ½ cup olive oil in a large non-stick frying pan. Add ½ the onions and ½ the garlic and ginger and cook until the onion is soft and pink. Then add the chopped ham, parsley, chilli and pepper powders. After the onions and ham are well cooked, add the tomatoes, sugar, the remaining onions and garlic and the tomato sauce. Allow to simmer until you have a smooth sauce, then add the white wine. Simmer for 10-12 minutes.

3. Gently mix in the boiled, salted basmati rice into half the sauce and mix well.

4. Stuff the squid hoods with the above mixture and stitch up the open sides with needle and thread.

5. Heat ½ cup of oil in a non-stick frying pan and fry the stuffed squid hoods till golden brown on both sides. Place them in a large pan or pyrex dish and pour the remainder of the sauce over all the stuffed hoods. Place the dish in an oven at 350°F for over an hour. Serve hot at once.

Fish Sticks Wrapped in Bacon and Fried in Batter

Seer fish are prime fish and very much in demand, both fresh and cured. They have white flesh with a high fat content.

Seer fishes are called Scomberomorinae, the family is Scombroidae.

The Seer has an elongated body, and hardly any scales. It has a wide mouth with strong teeth.

Preparation time: 45 mins   Cooking time: 1 Hour   Serves: 30

Ingredients

60 sticks of boneless surmai fish as thick as a finger

60 strips streaky bacon

Egg batter, made of egg, cornflour water, salt and pepper

Juice of 8 sour limes

Salt

Pepper

Oil

Method

1. Wash and marinade the fish fingers in salt, pepper and sour lime juice and set aside.

2. Take 1 piece of streaky bacon, remove the rind and wrap it around a fish finger and secure with toothpicks. Complete all the fingers in the same manner.

3. Make a batter with 4 eggs, 1 cup cornflour, water, salt and pepper. Mix the batter till smooth, leaving no lumps.

4. Heat oil in a large frying pan. Dip the fish fingers in the batter first and then deep fry till golden over a medium flame. Serve hot.

Surmai Slices in a Sweet-sour Green Sauce

Preparation time: 15 mins   Cooking time: 25 mins   Serves: 6

Ingredients

8 surmai slices without any holes
1 onion, pulped
Juice of 3 sour limes
1½ tbsps sugar
1 tsp cornflour
Salt
Sunflower oil

For the ground masala paste
(Grind fine in a little water)
1 cup fresh coriander leaves
6 green chillies, deseeded
4 large garlic cloves
1 tsp coriander seeds, broiled
1 tsp cumin seeds, broiled
1 tsp fennel seeds, broiled

Method

1. Wash the surmai slices and salt them.
2. Mix the cornflour in half a cup of water.
3. Heat 3 tablespoons of oil in a large flat vessel. When hot, add the pulped onion and cook till golden coloured.
4. Add the ground masala and cornflour water to it and cook for 5 minutes, stirring all the time till you have a thick mixture. Then add the fish pieces in a line and stir the vessel from side to side, holding it with 2 kitchen napkins. Pour ½ cup of water, shake well and taste for salt.
5. Allow the fish to cook well. Then pour the sugar and lime juice mixed well, and remove immediately from the fire.
6. Serve with black masoor dal and crisp bread or roti.

Surmai Sliced Pickle

Preparation time: 15 mins   Cooking time: 40 mins   Serves: 20

Ingredients

20 perfect Surmai slices without holes, 2" to 2½" in size

3 tbsps turmeric powder

2 tbsps black pepper powder

2 tbsps amchoor powder

5 cups vinegar

1 cup jaggery

4 sprigs curry leaves

Sea-salt, crushed

Sesame oil

For the ground masala paste

(Ground in sugarcane vinegar)

24 red chillies, deseeded

10 green chillies, deseeded

3 tbsps cumin seeds

18 large garlic cloves

1 tbsp mustard seeds

4 tbsps red chilli powder

Method

1.   Wash the fish twice and salt it and then apply the chilli, turmeric, black pepper and amchoor powders. Keep aside for 30 minutes.

2.   Heat oil on a very large griddle and allow it to smoke. Lower the heat and fry the fish slices in small batches and set aside in a large tray. Allow to cool.

3.   Place 3 cups of fresh oil in a very large flat-bottomed vessel on medium heat. When the oil starts smoking, add the curry leaves and lower the flame. Add the ground masala and stir for 5 minutes till it is well blended with the oil. Cook for 5 more minutes and then add the vinegar and the jaggery. Allow the mixture to boil for 7 minutes. Taste for salt. Remove the vessel from the stove and cool the gravy.

4.   Arrange the pieces of fried fish in a large glass jar. Pour the cold masala gravy over the pieces and shake the jar. The gravy should be well over 1" above the pieces. Close the bottle tight and keep it in a cool, dark place. The pickle should be ready to eat in 10 days.

Panzanella with Little Filleted Bits of White Fish

Preparation time: 15-20 mins   Cooking time: 35-40 mins   Serves: 6

Ingredients

400 gms filleted white fish (ghol, pomfret or surmai) cut into 1" cubes and washed twice

10 slices of bread, cut into 1" cubes

400 gms of large red tomatoes, skinned and cut finely

2 green capsicums, cut julienne

2 tbsps parsley or fresh coriander, finely chopped

3 sweet, deseeded green chillies, finely chopped

1 tsp ginger, finely chopped

2 tsps paprika

1 tsp black pepper, ground

½ tsp dried sage, crushed

½ tsp dried basil, crushed

Juice of 2 sour limes

2 eggs

2 tbsps cornflour

Salt

Olive oil or Sunflower oil

Method

1.   Wash the fish fillets twice and marinate them in salt, black pepper powder and lime juice for 1 hour.

2.   Mix the eggs and cornflour in a large bowl. Add the fish to it and mix well.

3.   Take a large frying pan and fill it half way with olive oil or sunflower oil. When hot, drop the bread cubes one at a time into the boiling oil so they do not stick together. Fry in small lots until they are golden brown and remove from the fire.

4.   In the same hot oil, drop the fish cubes one at a time. Fry in several small batches so they do not stick together. Remove from the hot oil when golden brown.

5.   In a clean frying pan add 2 tablespoons of the same oil and lightly fry the chillies, capsicums, ginger and after 2 minutes, add the finely chopped tomatoes. Add salt and the paprika and crushed sage and basil. Heat through for 5 minutes.

6.   Take a large glass bowl. Put in the fried bread cubes and the fish fillets.

7.   Then pour the cooked tomato mixture over it and mix well lightly. Serve immediately as a light brunch or lunch item or a first course for dinner.

Fish Cakes

Either salmon, ghol or surmai can be used to make these fish cakes.

Preparation time: 20 mins   Cooking time: 20-25 mins   Serves: 8-10

Ingredients

2 cups mashed potato

2 cups any white fish, boiled and flaked

7 green chillies, deseeded

Juice of 2 sour limes

3 tsps sugar

Eggs

Breadcrumbs

Salt

Sunflower oil

For the ground masala paste

(Grind fine and mix well)

½ cup fresh coriander leaves

8 large garlic cloves

1 tbsp broiled coriander seeds

1 ½ tsps broiled cumin seeds

10 black pepper corns

2 green cardamom seeds

Method

1.   Place the mashed potatoes in a tray. Sprinkle a little fine salt over them and mix in the ground masala. Then lightly add the flaked fish and mix everything thoroughly. Taste for salt.

2.   Mix the lime juice and sugar well, and add to the above mixture.

3.   Make 16 balls out of the fish mixture. Place breadcrumbs on a wooden board. Roll the fish balls in the crumbs and then flatten the top and bottom with a broad knife and form into round cake shapes.

4.   Whisk 2 eggs at a time in a soup plate.

5.   Half fill a frying pan with oil and place it on medium heat. When the oil heats up, dip the fish cakes in the egg and fry 3 to 5 of them at a time till golden brown.

6.   Serve hot with a green salad, black lentils, beans or any vegetable for lunch or dinner.

Turkish Swordfish Fillet – Kababs with Walnut Sauce

Preparation time: 35 mins   Cooking time: 55 mins   Serves: 8

Ingredients

700 gms of swordfish or shark fish or ghol fish fillets cut into 1" cubes

2-3 tsps red chilli powder

10 garlic cloves, crushed

½ cup coriander, chopped

¼ cup juice of fresh ginger

2 tsps black pepper powder

Fresh bay leaves

Juice of 2 sour limes

¼ cup olive oil or any other oil

Salt

For the Walnut Sauce:

110 gms shelled walnuts

6 cloves garlic

2 large slices of white bread – crust removed

½ tsp cumin powder

Juice of 1 sour lime

Salt

¾ cup olive oil or any other oil

Method

1.   Place the olive oil and sour lime juice in a big bowl and beat together until blended. Add the chilli powder, crushed garlic, pepper, chopped coriander, ginger juice and mix well.

2.   Salt the fish pieces and add them to the bowl containing the marinade and gently mix to coat all the fish pieces with it. Chill overnight in the refrigerator.

3.   To make the walnut sauce, grind the walnuts, garlic and salt till a thick paste is obtained. Soak the bread slices in water for 3 minutes. Squeeze the slices and add into the walnut paste. Mix the oil and lime juice together and add to the walnut paste. Blend all items, in the liquidizer. Taste for salt.

4.   Heat coals in the tandoor 15 minutes before the meal. Skewer the fish pieces onto each "seek" or kabab stick with a bay leaf between each piece. Roast over red hot coals. Baste the fish with any marinade which remains.

5.   When the fish pieces are roasted, serve them immediately with the walnut sauce.

The Tuna Fish

The Tunas are included in the order Perciformes, family Scombroidae. They have robust bodies, dark heads and are blackish blue. This fish is found in the Atlantic, the Indian and Pacific Oceans, South Africa, the Gulf of Aden, Lakshadweep, Sri Lanka and Australia.

This fish is exported to Japan where it is very popular.

Salad Nicoise with Tuna and Anchovies

Preparation time: 30 mins   Cooking time: Nil   Serves: 6-8

Ingredients

1 large tin or 2 small tins tuna fish

1 small tin anchovy fillets

500 gms boiled potatoes, skinned and diced

200 gms frenchbeans, cut diagonally and boiled in salted water (add a pinch of soda-bi-carb to retain its green colour)

1 capsicum, deseeded and cut into very fine strips

1 red or golden pepper, deseeded and cut into thin strips

8 baby tomatoes

1 cucumber, peeled and thinly sliced

16 black olives

3 hard boiled eggs, sliced thickly

1 iceberg lettuce – leaves washed and dried

Salt

For the Vinaigrette

1 tbsp made mustard

2 tsps freshly ground black pepper

3 large garlic cloves, well crushed

1½ tbsps each, fresh parsley, chives, celery, finely chopped

4 tsps sugar

2 tbsps balsamic vinegar or wine vinegar

2 tbsps sour lime juice

½ cup virgin olive oil

Salt

Method

1.   Drain the tuna and anchovy fillets and set aside.

2.   Arrange the lettuce leaves tastefully around a silver salver. Arrange the cucumber and egg slices on top of the leaves. Then add the, potatoes and frenchbeans.

3.   Make the vinaigrette by mixing all the items in a glass bowl and shaking well.

4.   Flake the tuna and pile it in the centre of the dish. Arrange the anchovies on top in a diamond pattern. Sprinkle with the capsicum and red or golden pepper strips.

5.   Arrange the cherry tomatoes and black olives all around the salad.

6.   Shake the vinaigrette once more and pour it over the salad. Chill. Serve at lunch time with French bread and butter.

Tuna Fish in Spicy Yoghurt Sauce

Preparation time: 10 mins   Cooking time: 25 mins   Serves: 6

Ingredients

8 medium sized tuna pieces
400 gms thick yoghurt
2 large onions, pulped
2 tbsps gram flour
1 tbsp sugar
2 split green chillies
2 sprigs curry leaves
Salt
Sesame oil

For the ground masala paste
(Grind fine with a little water)
9 red Kashmiri chillies
8 large cloves garlic
1 tbsp cumin seeds
1 tsp mustard seeds
½ cup coriander leaves, fresh chopped

Method

1.   Wash and salt the tuna fish and set aside.

2.   Put the onions and 3 tablespoons oil in a vessel on medium heat. Add the curry leaves. When the onion turns brown, add the ground masala and fry for 5 minutes. Add salt and ½ cup water. Bring to a boil, add the green chillies and set down from the stove.

3.   Fry the tuna fish lightly in hot oil and set aside.

4.   Whisk the yoghurt along with the sugar and gram flour mixed in a little water.

5.   Replace the gravy on the stove over medium heat. Add the yoghurt and mix non-stop till it is well assimilated in the gravy. Taste for salt. When the gravy is bubbling, add the fried tuna pieces and boil the gravy for 5 minutes. Shake the vessel from side to side and remove from the fire.

6.   Serve immediately with ghee rice or khichdi or vegetable pulao.

Trout in a Sweet Sour Sauce

Preparation time: 10 mins   Cooking time: 25 mins   Serves: 4-6

Ingredients

6 medium trout kept whole, clean the body and remove the gills and entrails. Keep the heads and tails intact. Wash thoroughly twice.

2 small onions, finely chopped

1 cup tomato juice

½ cup vinegar

½ cup sugar

1 tbsp cracked black pepper

1 tsp garlic, finely chopped

1 tsp ginger, finely chopped

3 sprigs fresh rosemary – if not available, 1 tsp dried rosemary

1½ tbsps self-raising flour

Salt

Extra Virgin Olive oil or Peanut oil

Method

1.   Heat ½ cup of olive oil in a large frying pan. Apply salt and cracked pepper to the trouts and fry them till golden brown. Fry in 2 batches and set aside.

2.   Place the excess oil in a saucepan and heat. When the oil heats up, add the onions, garlic and ginger and cook till the onions are pink and soft.

3.   Add the flour, stir well and cook for 3 minutes. Then add the vinegar, tomato juice and sugar and stir well. Let the sauce boil and bubble before removing from the fire. Taste for salt.

4.   Place the sauce in a large rectangular pyrex dish. Carefully, place the trout on it. Add the rosemary on top of the fish.

5.   Heat in a low oven at 250°F for 10 to 12 minutes.

6.   Serve with jacket potatoes and a cucumber-yoghurt raita.